JOHN ADAMS
AND THE DIPLOMACY
OF THE AMERICAN
REVOLUTION

JAMES H. HUTSON

JOHN ADAMS
AND THE DIPLOMACY
OF THE AMERICAN
REVOLUTION

THE UNIVERSITY PRESS OF KENTUCKY

FOR KATHY

Library of Congress Cataloging in Publication Data

Hutson, James H

   John Adams and the diplomacy of the American
Revolution

   Bibliography: p.
   Includes Index.
   1. United States—Foreign relations—Revolution,
1775–1783   2. Adams, John, Pres. U. S., 1735–
1826.   I. Title.
E249.H87   973.3'2'0924   79-57575
ISBN 0-8131-1404-7

Scholarly publisher for the Commonwealth
serving Berea College, Centre College of Kentucky,
Eastern Kentucky University, The Filson Club,
Georgetown College, Kentucky Historical Society,
Kentucky State University, Morehead State University,
Murray State University, Northern Kentucky University,
Transylvania University, University of Kentucky,
University of Louisville, and Western Kentucky University.

Editorial and Sales Offices: Lexington, Kentucky 40506

CONTENTS

ACKNOWLEDGMENTS

Edmund S. Morgan, Sterling Professor of History, Yale University, has read and criticized this manuscript twice and has encouraged me to publish it. Without his assistance and moral support at critical periods, it would have never become a book. Stephen G. Kurtz, now principal of Phillips Exeter Academy, also helped me by interrupting his busy schedule and giving the manuscript a tough-minded reading. Several other people have assisted me in ways of which they, perhaps, were not aware: Mr. and Mrs. David Hutson, Mrs. Joseph Hranac, Gayle and Tracey Weber, and Benjamin and Scott Hutson. I am grateful for the opportunity of working at an institution as hospitable to ideas as the Library of Congress and would like, in particular, to acknowledge the intellectual stimulation supplied by my colleagues in the Manuscript Division.

CHAPTER 1

FORMULATING AN
AMERICAN FOREIGN POLICY

The foreign policy of the American Revolution was not revolutionary. The ideas shaping it were those that informed European diplomatic thinking throughout the eighteenth century. Colonial Americans adopted those ideas as readily as they did the fashions, the books, and the other appurtenances of European culture that they imported so avidly. John Adams and his fellow statesmen of the Revolution absorbed the ideas as they grew up and, in 1776, applied them to the new American nation's relations with foreign powers.

Eighteenth-century European diplomacy, writes Felix Gilbert, was "entirely dominated by the concept of power." Its key ideas were the balance of power, which apologists promoted as an enlightened mechanism to secure peace, and "the doctrine of the interest of states," according to which interest was the sole arbiter of political action.[1] The economic theory underpinning eighteenth-century diplomacy was mercantilism, which measured national power by national wealth and considered commerce as the source of both.[2] The eighteenth century broadened the balance of power to include colonies and affirmed that colonial commerce was the decisive counter in the balance. French Foreign Minister Choiseul summarized this outlook in 1759:

"The true balance of power really resides in commerce and America."[3]

A diplomacy based on power was congenial to eighteenth-century Americans because they subscribed to a theory of politics, propounded by English Opposition writers, which stressed that "the ultimate explanation of every political controversy was the disposition of power." The sensitivity of colonial Americans to power was, according to a leading expositor of their ideas, "one of the most striking things" in their thinking.[4] Even had colonial Americans never heard of the English Opposition, they would have been attentive to power in politics because of their long conflict with the French. The object of the wars with France was dominion—power over the North American continent. Therefore, an appreciation of power in politics was natural for the colonists.

In soliciting British assistance against the French, the colonists invoked religion and morality far less than self-interest and power, for they correctly assumed that British statesmen were more likely to be moved by calculations of power than by reminders of religious affinity. At every crisis with the French, Americans stressed to the British that they could not afford to lose the colonies because they were the source of their national power and of their weight in the European balance. James Logan's "Of the State of the British Plantations in America" demonstrates that Americans had perfected this kind of appeal by 1732. Logan's paper was laced with references to the "true Interest," the "present Interest," of Britain and her European competitors. And it insisted that Britain's power and her position in the European balance was derived from America. "The principal Security of Britain," wrote Logan, "consists in its Naval force and this is supported by its Trade and Navigation. [It is no] less certain that these are very much advanced by means of the British Dominions in America; the Preservation of which is therefore of the utmost importance to the Kingdom itself, for it is manifest that if France could possess itself of those Do-

minions and thereby become Masters of all their Trade
. . . they would soon be an Overmatch in Naval Strength to
the rest of Europe, and then be in a Condition to prescribe
Laws to the whole." "The American Plantations," Logan concluded, "are of such Importance to Britain, that the Loss of
them to any other Power, especially to France might be its own
ruin."[5]

King George's War (the War of the Austrian Succession) produced the customary American appeals to Britain: " 'All parts of
the Empire were interdependent,' " wrote Massachusettensis in
1746, " 'and if the Colonies were lost . . . Britain would lose its
own independence too.' "[6] American balance-of-power arguments reached a crescendo during the early years of the French
and Indian War, when the apparently unprecedented gravity of
the French threat produced scores of anxious affirmations of
America's importance to Britain. Taking their cue, perhaps,
from Dr. John Mitchell, who in 1757 declared that "interest
rules all the world. Why should it not rule in the Colonies,"[7]
Americans vied with one another in emphasizing interest as the
motive force of politics and in asserting their importance to the
European balance of power. In a sermon preached to the Massachusetts General Court on May 29, 1754, Jonathan Mayhew asserted that the "liberties of Europe" depended on the outcome
of the struggle with the French, "for of so great consequence is
the empire of North America . . . that it must turn the scale of
power greatly in the favour of the only Monarch, from whom
those liberties are in danger; and against the Prince, who is the
grand support and bulwark of them." The next year the Pennsylvania cartographer Lewis Evans predicted that the possession
of the Ohio Country "will make so great an addition to that Nation which wins it, where there is no third State to hold the Ballance of Power, that the Loser must inevitably sink under his
Rival." According to Doctor William Clarke of Boston, writing
in the same year, "These Colonies are of such Consequence to
the Trade, Wealth and Naval Power of Great-Britain, and will in

future Time make so much larger Additions to it, that whilst she keep them entire, she will be able to maintain not only her Independency, but her Superiority as a Maritime Power. And on the other Hand, should she once lose them, and the French gain them, Great Britain herself must necessarily be reduced to an absolute Subjection to the French Crown, to nothing more than a Province of France."[8] Americans, it is apparent, endorsed the conviction of European diplomacy, that "they controlled the balance of power among the various colonizing nations" and "that whichever nation controlled North America would hold the hegemony of power over the rest of Europe."[9]

Most of the leaders of the American Revolution matured during the French and Indian War—John Adams graduated from college the month of Braddock's defeat—and they adopted as their own the attitude toward foreign affairs which prevailed during that period. Since few statements by leaders of the Revolution survive from the 1750s, the proof of this contention must principally rest on the similarity between the foreign-policy assumptions of the Revolution and of the French and Indian War. John Adams is unusual in that he left statements about his youthful attitude toward foreign affairs which show the continuity of his views between the 1750s and the 1770s.

From a tender age Adams was thrilled by the prospects of American power. At ten he thought the men of Massachusetts a race of heroes, who would have "cut to pieces at once the Duke D'Enville's army" had it dared attack Boston. In 1755 so great was his "confidence in the resolution of my countrymen, that I had no doubt we could defend ourselves against the French, and that better without England than with her." Adams's youthful cockiness fed upon a vision of American greatness which was widely held in the colonies and which was nothing less than a belief—decades before scholars usually locate it—in the country's manifest destiny. New Englanders believed—"with rapture," Adams recalled later in life—that the Pilgrim Fathers had chiseled into Plymouth Rock the prophecy:

The eastern nations sink, their glory ends
An empire rises where the sun descends

"There is nothing . . . more ancient in my memory," he wrote, "than the observation that arts, sciences, and empire had travelled westward; and in conversation it was always added, since I was a child, that the next leap would be over the Atlantic into America."[10]

Benjamin Franklin documented this American dream in 1751 with his *Observations concerning the Increase of Mankind*, which showed that the population of the colonies was doubling every twenty years and would continue to do so into the indefinite future. Here was scientific confirmation that America's vision of imperial destiny could become a reality, for a people increasing at the rate Franklin predicted, over a land mass as large as the North American continent, would become a colossus. The impact of the *Observations* on Adams is demonstrated by his letter to Nathan Webb, October 12, 1755: "Soon after the Reformation a few people came over into this new world for Conscience sake. Perhaps this (apparently) trivial incident, may transfer the great seat of Empire into America. It looks likely to me. For if we can remove the turbulent Gallicks, our People according to the exactest Computations, will in another Century, become more numerous than England itself. Should this be the Case, since we have (I may say) all the naval stores of the Nation in our hands, it will be easy to obtain the mastery of the seas, and then the united force of all Europe, will not be able to subdue us."[11] His faith supported by Franklin's facts, Adams sounded a theme that echoed across the colonies in the next two decades and that helped dictate the shape of Revolutionary foreign policy: the "mighty empire" theme.

References to a mighty empire in America, sustained by a cornucopia of people and land, abound in the writings of the colonists from the mid-1750s onward. In 1759, for example, the Reverend Jonathan Mayhew preached of a "mighty empire . . . in numbers little inferior to perhaps the greatest in

Europe, and in felicity to none." Traveling through the colonies in the same year, the English clergyman Andrew Burnaby marveled that "an idea, strange as it is visionary, has entered into the minds of the generality of mankind, that empire is travelling westward"; the colonists, he noted, were "looking forward with eager and impatient expectation to that destined moment when America is to give law to the rest of the world." In 1767 Franklin predicted that "America, an immense territory, favoured by Nature with all advantages of climate, soil, great navigable rivers, and lakes, must become a great country, populous and mighty." In 1772 Arthur Lee exulted that America "like a young phoenix . . . will rise plumed and glorious from her mother's ashes"; a "little time" must "lay the most permanent foundation of population and power. America, in her turn, will be the imperial mistress of the world." From 1774 until the Declaration of Independence the mighty empire theme played as often as a popular song. "It requires but a small portion of the gift of discernment," wrote Samuel Adams on April 4, 1774, "for anyone to foresee, that providence will erect a mighty empire in America." Benjamin Rush spoke of America's "future populousness and grandeur"; Alexander Hamilton, of its "dawning splendour"; Jacob Duché, of its "rising glory"; and James Warren, of its "rising Empire." With a patronizing benevolence, William Hooper hoped that when "that Change comes and come it must, that America must become the seat of Empire, may Britain gently verge down the decline of life, and sink away in the arms of her American Sons."[12]

The consciousness of American power puffed up many members of the Continental Congress into a swaggering, "haughty Temper"—"I do verily believe that N. America will give law to that proud imperious Island," exclaimed Richard Henry Lee on April 1, 1776—and, for a time, gave congressional proceedings a jingoist tone. "We are too haughty to look to God," complained Zubly of Georgia on October 24, 1775, and "rather talk of presenting Law to a Conquered people than defending ourselves under great disadvantages against one of the greatest forces of the universe." Zubly's strictures differed little from those of the Tories, who, as early as 1768, reproved the Whigs for growing "more imperious, haughty, nay insolent every day," "so intoxicated with their own importance," so full of "omnipotency and all-sufficientcy."[13]

John Adams stood foremost among those whom General Gage criticized for "presumption [and] arrogance" in flaunting American power. At no time before or during the Revolutionary War did he waver from his 1755 conviction that America was a match for the "united force" of Europe. His favorite metaphor for the rising American empire was "young Hercules," whose ability to strangle the British serpent in its cradle he never doubted. Everywhere his correspondence breathes the absolute conviction of America's "unconquerability." Using "Dr. Franklin's rule of progression" Adams calculated that "near twenty thousand fighting men [were] added to the numbers in America every year." The colonies were "at such distances from one another" and "such a multitude of posts" would be "necessary to be garrisoned and provided in order to command any one Colony" that he calculated that "an army of a hundred thousand men would soon find itself consumed in getting and keeping possession of one or two" of them. Consequently, he was certain that "the Thirteen Colonies . . . leagued together in a faithfull Confederacy might bid Defiance to all the Potentates of Europe if united against them" (March 23, 1776), might "sustain the War, for thirty years to come, better than France, Spain, or England" (April 26, 1780), might be confident that it was "impossible for any, the proudest of them, to conquer us" (May 8, 1785). Adams, quite simply, was convinced that the United States would become the "greatest Power on Earth" and that "within the Life of Man." His conviction of American power was the key to his thinking about foreign policy.[14]

As their fathers and grandfathers had done, the statesmen of the American Revolution considered the plenitude of American power in the context of the European balance of power; Adams, for example, told a Dutch merchant in 1778 that he had been educated from his cradle in balance-of-power thinking.[15] Revolutionary statesmen, however, were better equipped than James Logan or William Clarke to substantiate their claims that the colonies were the decisive factor in British power and, by extension, in the European balance, for they had figures showing precisely how the dynamics of American demography supported British commerce, that "modern source of wealth and power," as Jefferson expressed it in good mercantilistic fashion. Some Americans, like Arthur Lee, made what seemed to be the reasonable assumption that American population and British commerce increased in proportion. "With the growth of the Colonies and in exact proportion," Lee lectured a British audience, "must your Trade, your Marine, your Revenue, your Riches grow." But Lee was wrong. Franklin produced figures in 1760 showing that British trade to the colonies grew four times faster than American population; in 1774 the First Continental Congress had figures, derived from more detailed records, showing the increase to be three times the rate of population growth. These numbers never failed to work Americans up to a pitch of excitement, for they appeared to confirm that the colonies were the engine of British power. Franklin was transported by the statistics: "What an Accession of Power to the British Empire by Sea as well as by Land! What Increase of Trade and Navigation! What Numbers of Ships and Seamen!" Obviously, "the foundation of the future grandeur and stability of the British empire lie in America." Other Americans picked up this refrain. "The Foundations of the Power and Glory of Great Britain are Based in America," claimed John Dickinson in 1765. America, declared George Wythe in 1774, "is one of the Wings upon which the British Eagle has soared to the Skies." The union of Britain with America has raised her, the Second Continental Congress affirmed, "to a power the most extraordinary the world had ever known."[16]

Americans agreed, then, that they were the source of Britain's power and of her position in the European balance. Arguing in 1773 that Britain was "worth preserving," Franklin pointed the moral of his statistics: "Her weight in the scale of Europe, and her safety in a great degree, may depend on our union with her." A year later, the Doctor's antagonist but former friend and fellow imperial strategist at the Albany Congress of 1754, Thomas Hutchinson, calculated the loss of America on Britain's position vis-à-vis France. Repeating the words of William Clarke in 1755, Hutchinson warned: "Give up the colonies to a foreign power and run the risk of making this kingdom a province of the same power."[17] The balance of power was the framework in which Americans at all points on the political spectrum considered foreign affairs. The Loyalist Daniel Leonard scoffed at Whig pretensions; in his view, the colonies were merely "the light dust of the balance." Whigs like Hugh Williamson speculated about the colonies being thrown "into the other scale." The Loyalist Charles Inglis, the literary adversary of *Common Sense*, predicted that European powers would prevent France from intervening on America's behalf because they were "too jealous of her—too deeply interested in preserving a due ballance of power, which is a principal object in European politics." Elbridge Gerry, on the other hand, thought that the European balance would work in the United States' favor. "It is acknowledged on all hands," wrote Gerry on November 11, 1776, "that now is the Time for France and Spain to destroy the Balance of power which has been heretofore said to be preserved in Europe, but considered as preponderating against them." Summarizing the assumptions on which all foreign policy arguments were based, Samuel Adams wrote on February 4, 1777: "The War between Britain and the United States of America will affect the Ballance of Power in Europe. Will not the different Powers take different sides to adjust the Ballance to their different Interests?"[18]

Americans of the Revolutionary generation thought of foreign affairs in terms of the balance of power not simply because it was the inherited mode of analysis but because they genuinely believed that it was a progressive principle in international affairs. The Reverend John Witherspoon articulated this view in a speech to Congress, July 30, 1776, in which he listed various signs of "progress . . . in the order and perfection of human society." Among these were religious freedom and the balance of power. "It is," said Witherspoon, "but little above two hundred years since that enlarged system called the balance of power took place; and I maintain, that it is a greater step from the former disunited and hostile situation of kingdoms and states, to their present condition, than it would be from their present condition to a state of more perfect and lasting union."[19]

John Adams saw as clearly as any man in the colonies that the mighty empire rising in America had made Britain mighty, that "the English by means of their commerce and extensive settlements abroad, arose to a degree of opulence and naval power" which was awesome. It followed that a "Connection with America must in the future decide the Ballance of Maritime Power in Europe."[20] In fact, Adams believed that were Britain and America to remain united, were Britain to retain control over America's expanding population and commerce, the European balance would be destroyed. "If Great Britain and America should ever be again united under one domination," he wrote in 1780, "there would be an end of the liberty of all other nations upon the seas. All commerce and navigation of the world would be swallowed up in one frightful despotism." France's "existence as a maritime and commercial power" would be destroyed, as would Spain's and the Netherlands'. The indivisible British Empire "would establish an absolute tyranny upon the ocean," would realize the ancient dream of despots by becoming a "universal Monarchy."[21] On the other hand, Adams believed that were France and Spain to monopolize American commerce, the balance would be turned as apocalyptically against Britain. Such a development, Adams wrote as if he were a Briton, would "ruin our credit, destroy our manufactures, reduce to nothing our influence in Europe, [and] depress our naval power to such an inferiority to France and Spain as we shall never recover." Such a loss would be "fatal" to Britain, a diagnosis in which Adams's colleagues agreed.[22] So, too, did the British ministry, which, in the words of a recent student, feared that the loss of America would lead to "the collapse of the power system which enabled the British nation to compete on equal if not superior terms in the international jungle." Or, as the Earl of Carlisle predicted in 1776, if Britain lost America she would "sink into obscurity and insignificance, falling at length a prey to the first powerful or ambitious state, which may meditate a conquest of this island."[23] That Britons agreed with American perceptions of their contribution to the Empire's strength illustrates the conformity of American and European presumptions about the role of colonies in the balance of power.

The letter from Adams to Webb, October 12, 1755, reveals an intellectual climate in which that other staple of power politics, an emphasis on interest, flourished. "The whole town [Worcester]," Adams wrote, "is immers'd in Politicks. The interests of Nations, and all the dira of War, make the subject of every Conversation."[24] Adams never relinquished the practice of resolving domestic and foreign politics into considerations of interest. "Reason, justice and equity never had weight enough on the face of the earth," he lectured the Continental Congress in July 1776, "to govern the councils of men, it is interest alone which does it, and it is interest alone which can be trusted." Four years later he wrote: "No attachment between Nations arising merely from a Similarity of Laws and Government is ever very strong or sufficient to bind Nations together who have opposite or even different Interests."[25] Adams found it difficult to imagine foreign-policy decisions being based on any other calculation than interest. His contemporaries shared his attitude. As Samuel Adams wrote James Warren on April 17, 1777: "When it suits the Interest of foreign Powers they will aid us substantially. That some of them will find it their Interest to aid us I can hardly doubt but there seems not to be Virtue enough left in the World from generous and disinterested Motives to interpose in support of the Common Rights of Mankind."[26]

There was, then, a consensus about foreign policy among Revolutionary Americans, a consensus formed around the classical European diplomatic concepts of the balance of power and the interests of states, concepts that flourished in the colonies from the early years of the eighteenth century. The events of the Revolution interacted with these attitudes to create the foreign policy of the new American nation. Describing the creation of that foreign policy is not easy, however, because the documentary record is poor. Public advocacy of a foreign policy presupposes a commitment to national independence. Until the beginning of 1776, however, most Americans wanted reconciliation with Great Britain. Therefore, although they may have ruminated about the shape of an independent foreign policy and may have shared their thoughts with their friends, they did not, in most cases, put them on the public record. Furthermore, the secrecy rule in the Continental Congress restrained most delegates from revealing what was said about foreign affairs there. The inhibiting effect of the congressional rule was explained by John Adams on March 18, 1777: "I am under such Injunctions and Engagements to communicate nothing relative to foreign affairs that I ought not to do it." The meagerness of the resulting record has led some scholars to conclude that Revolutionary statesmen were not interested in foreign policy or ignored the subject because they abhorred it: "The entire colonial experience made foreign policy alien and repulsive to Americans," wrote Felix Gilbert.[27] This is not true. Evidence left by the Loyalists and incidental remarks by Whigs show that as early as the fall of 1774 there was an informed dialogue in the colonies about foreign policy.

The actions of the First Continental Congress, although taken in good faith to produce a reconciliation with Britain, alarmed many men who subsequently became Loyalists. They believed

that the Congress had set the colonies on the high road to independence without any appreciation of the dangers involved. Independence, they claimed, posed unacceptable risks for the
colonies by depriving them of British protection and throwing
them into an arena of amoral, rapacious states. "If we declare for
Independency," they argued, "Britain will not for time to come,
protect us against other nations, and we shall in time, and probably very soon, become a prey to the French and Spaniards, or
some other enemy."[28] The Loyalists vigorously pressed this assertion at every stage of the debate over independence and many
moderates used it as well. It raised the fundamental question of
whether national self-preservation was possible for a young republic in a world of predatory monarchies. This was the central
issue in all discussions of foreign affairs up to and beyond the
Declaration of Independence.

The Loyalist message was always the same: the world that
an independent United States would inhabit was a jungle.
"As matters are now circumstanced throughout Christendom,"
wrote Charles Inglis, "no state can preserve its independency
without a standing army. The nation that would neglect to keep
one, and a naval force, if it has any sea coast, must infallibly fall
a prey to some of its ambitious and more vigilant neighbors."
"Should it be known abroad that Great-Britain had withdrawn
her protection," asserted Thomas Chandler in the fall of 1774,
"within the compass of one year our sea-ports would be ravaged,
and our vessels plundered as soon as they left our harbours." The
most lurid example of the savagery of international affairs, the
Loyalists reminded their fellow Americans, was the partition of
Poland in 1772. "The practice of conquering and dividing territories and kingdoms is become fashionable in Europe," warned
Joseph Galloway at the conclusion of the First Continental Congress. An independent America, cautioned Daniel Leonard on
January 30, 1775, would become an "easy prey, and would be
parcelled out, Poland like."[29] None of the Loyalists expected
that the "three crowned sinners"—Russia, Prussia, and

Austria—who had despoiled Poland would pounce on the colonies. Rather they anticipated danger from the hereditary enemies of America, France and Spain, still smarting from the loss of territories "that were torn, reluctant and bleeding from them in the last war by the superior strength of Britain."[30] "The ambition of France is still alive and active," asserted Galloway. "America is daily growing a more alluring object of her ambition. Her fleets, and those of her natural ally, the King of Spain, are increasing. . . . Under this prospect of things, what can America expect, while she denies the authority of the mother-state; and by that denial incurs a forfeiture of her protection . . . she must in all probability soon become the slave of arbitrary power—of Popish bigotry and superstition." Even if France and Spain did not conquer and divide the colonies by main force, the Loyalists predicted that these courts, so notorious for address and intrigue, would gain control by negotiations, for if an independent America treated with them, she would be overreached and subjugated. The protection of the Bourbons, declared Thomas Chandler in the fall of 1774, could be obtained only "on terms not of our proposing, but of theirs." "We can make them no return for protection but by trade," wrote Leonard on January 30, 1775, and "of that they can have no assurance, unless we become subject to their laws."[31]

The Whigs felt the full force of the Loyalist arguments. They knew that international politics were brutal: "The passions of despotism," wrote John Dickinson in May 1774, "raging like a plague, about seven years past, have spread with unusual malignity through Europe. Corsica, Poland, and Sweden have sunk beneath it." The partition of Poland made a profound and lasting impression on them—the *Federalist* dilated upon it, Adams and Jefferson discussed it as late as 1816—and they yielded to no one in their distrust of France; Adams, for example, was never able to rid himself of prejudices imbibed as a youth against that "ambitious and faithless Nation," as he called her at age twenty-one. Therefore, the burden of proof was always on the Whigs to prove that independence would not cause the country to be devoured by a foreign enemy.[32]

Their first line of defense against this fear was their confidence in the power of America, their faith in the strength of the "mighty empire." In ridiculing Whig pretensions in the fall of 1774, Thomas Chandler revealed their scope: according to Chandler, the "ignorant and deluded American" contended that "notwithstanding all that can be said of the naval strength of Great Britain, it is asserted by our patriotic leaders, and we have reason to think, that the Colonies of themselves, are able to withstand all her force." Replying to Daniel Leonard on February 6, 1775, John Adams brimmed with his usual confidence in American power: "In a land war, this continent might defend itself against all the world. We have men enough, and those men have as good natural understandings and as much natural courage as any other men."[33] The Whig rejoinder to Loyalist warnings was set by early 1775: America had adequate power to sustain herself as an independent nation.

In the fall of 1774 Whigs displayed the characteristic American insight into how the power of the colonies affected the European balance of power. Britain, declared Richard Henry Lee at the First Continental Congress, "could not exist" without the commercial connection with America, the dissolution of which, the Second Continental Congress informed the people of Britain, would "deliver you, weak and defenceless, to your natural enemies." To detach America from Britain would, therefore, be a paramount interest of her rivals and no Whig doubted that the Bourbons would perceive this. Replying to the Loyalist Samuel Seabury in February 1775, Alexander Hamilton wrote: "A more desireable object, to France and Spain, than the disunion of these colonies from Great Britain, cannot be imagined. Every dictate of policy and interest would prompt them to forward it, by every possible means. They could not take any so effectual method, to destroy the growing power of their great rival."[34]

If the Bourbons destroyed Britain, would they turn on America next? The Whigs believed that, if they did, the others powers of Europe would intervene against them to preserve the balance of power. As early as the fall of 1774 the Whigs grasped what became the central feature of the foreign policy formulated by the independent United States two years later: that the European balance of power, if manipulated properly by America, would guarantee her national security. The proper way to manipulate the balance, it was perceived, was by establishing free trade between America and Europe. The Whigs claimed, Daniel Leonard declared on January 30, 1775, "that the colonies would open a free trade with all the world, and all nations would join in protecting their common mart." Leonard was describing what was a Whig article of faith throughout the struggle with Britain, a "favorite Maxim," as Dickinson expressed it in June 1776, "that our commerce is so valuable, it will protect itself."[35] What the Whigs meant was that American commerce was such a superb source of power that European nations would not permit one of their number to attack America and monopolize it lest the aggressor destroy the balance of power. A document in the Adams Papers, dated September 1774, discusses the situation from the perspective of any three European powers: "Neither of these powers, would suffer either of them, to engross this Country to themselves; for if they did, the Balance of Power would be so much against the other two, that they would not agree to it."[36] In contemplating a foreign policy for an independent nation, the Whigs believed, then, that they had two assets for national self-preservation: their country's power and the European balance of power.

The examination of foreign policy, which the meeting of the First Continental Congress provoked, seems to have subsided somewhat in the spring and summer of 1775. This, however, may be a false impression, produced by the absence of evidence rather than by the absence of attention to foreign affairs. The Second Continental Congress certainly discussed international relations, for in its Declaration of the Causes and Necessity for

Taking Up Arms, July 6, 1775, it confidently asserted that for-eign assistance was available, if the colonies chose to seek it.[37] Later in life Adams recalled that, at the beginning of the Second Congress, he had proposed a major foreign-policy initiative of which no evidence survives in contemporary documents. Adams recommended that British officials throughout the colonies be seized as hostages for the people of Boston, that new govern-ments be established in every colony, that independence be de-clared, and that negotiations then be initiated with Britain for a resolution of the problems dividing the two nations. "I was also," Adams stated, "for informing Great Britain very frankly that hitherto we were free but if the War should be continued, We were determined to seek Alliances with France, Spain, and any other Power of Europe." If negotiations with Britain were successful, the colonies would relinquish their independence and assume what Adams evidently conceived of as a position re-sembling the autonomy within the empire demanded by the First Continental Congress.[38] Britain, apparently, would be al-lowed to continue its monopoly of American trade. What discus-sions Adams's proposal produced is not known.

Consideration of foreign affairs quickened in the fall of 1775, as Congress debated opening the ports of America to the world. George III's refusal to respond to the Olive Branch Petition (July 8, 1775), considered by most delegates to be America's final of-fer of reconciliation, must have raised the question of indepen-dence and apparently caused some in Congress to warn that the partition Galloway and Leonard had predicted the preceding winter would be attempted, to assert that, rather than lose the colonies, Britain would purchase French and Spanish support by partitioning them with the Bourbon powers. George Wythe was evidently responding to such an argument on October 21 when he declared: "I know of no Instance where a Colony had revolted and a foreign Nation has interposed to subdue them. But many of the Contrary. If France and Spain should furnish Ships and Soldiers, England must pay them! Where are her Finances?"[39]

John Adams

It may also have been in response to the threat of a partition treaty that in November Samuel Chase, seconded by John Adams, moved that Congress send "Embassadors to France, with conditional Instructions." All that is known of this motion is Adams's statement on July 9, 1776, that it was "murdered, terminating in a Committee of secret correspondence, which came to nothing."[40] In his *Autobiography* Adams recorded the arguments he used to support an embassy to France. "Interest could not lie," he declared, and "the Interest of France was so obvious . . . that nothing but a judicial Infatuation of her Councils could restrain her from embracing Us." "It was the unquestionable Interest of France that the British continental Colonies should be independent," he continued, because Britain's exclusive possession of their manpower and commerce had exalted her "to a height of Power and Preeminence that France . . . could not endure." France's "Rank, her Consideration in Europe, and even her Safety and Independence were at stake." Were America to declare independence and offer France a commercial treaty, her self-interest would compel her to accept it, because the "Opening of American Trade to her would be a vast resource for her Commerce and Naval Power" and would enable her to redress the balance of power which had swung so dangerously in Britain's favor.[41] The conviction that France would be governed by interests which would dictate that she sever America from Britain—rather than join her in a partition that would enable Britain to retain a footing in the colonies—guided and comforted the Whigs as the debates on foreign policy became more intense in the early months of 1776.

Thomas Paine's sensational pamphlet *Common Sense*, published on January 10, 1776, urged Americans to declare themselves independent, because "it is the true interest of this continent to be so." According to Paine, an independent America would enjoy better relations with the international community than she would as a colonial auxiliary of a belligerent Britain. The success of *Common Sense* roused the Tories to employ what had become their familiar tactic of trying to frighten Americans out of independence by displaying the terrors of a Franco-Spanish partition treaty (which they could do with conviction since they genuinely believed that it might occur). At the beginning of February, Charles Inglis published his rebuttal to *Common Sense, The True Interest of America Impartially Stated*, in which he issued the following warning: "For my part, I should not in the least be surprised, if on such a prospect as the Independence of America, she [Great Britain] would parcel out this continent to the different European Powers. Canada might be restored to France, Florida to Spain, with additions to each. . . . Let no man think this chimerical or improbable. The independency of America would be so fatal to Britain, that she would leave nothing in her power undone to prevent it. I believe as firmly as I do my own existence, that if every other method failed, she would try some such expedient as this, to disconcert our scheme of independency; and let any man figure to himself the situation of these British colonies, if only Canada were restored to France." Later in the pamphlet, Inglis added: "Nay, further; I can whisper a secret to the author of Common Sense, provided he will let it go no further—which is—That France and Spain have *actually made an offer of their assistance* to Great Britain, in the present contest with the Colonies. This intelligence comes from such authority as would remove all doubt about the matter, even from our zealous Republican."[42]

Inglis's intelligence was apparently a *mémoire* concocted in London by a scheming French Jesuit, one Pierre Roubaud, who palmed it off on the British ministry as a demarche of the French ambassador, the Count de Guines. The *mémoire* purported to offer French assistance to Britain in crushing the American rebellion. Vergennes's agent, Garnier, informed him on March 1, 1776, that he was "persuaded that the British ministry is really imbued with the idea that we have pretended to make them offers to join ourselves to them in their project of exterminating the Americans, or subjugating them to the Metropolis." British officials sent Roubaud's *mémoire* to the colonies, "to convince the Americans that France, far from wishing to help them, was prepared to join itself to England to subjugate them." It was evidently Roubaud's *mémoire*, or some account of it, which emboldened Inglis to predict partition and other Tories like William Smith to invite Americans to "behold the face of Poland and visit the scenes of havock and desolation which mark the late footprints of the contending foreign powers in that country."[43] Tory scare tactics backfired; instead of frightening the Whigs out of independence, they hastened them toward it.

The Whigs gave full credence to the possibility of a partition treaty. By February 1776 the colonies, despite their recent reverse in Canada, appeared to be as strong militarily as their most ardent boosters had foretold. Therefore, if they were "impregnable" to British arms, as Thomas Lynch expressed it,[44] and at the same time indispensable to British security, it seemed likely that, rather than relinquish them, George III's ministers would share them with other foreign powers. No one doubted that the ministry was capable of offering such a deal or that the Bourbons were capable of accepting it. For years Americans had regarded the king's ministers as moral bankrupts, engaged in a sinister conspiracy to enslave them, and they had no trouble imagining them extending their operations to the Court of Versailles, which would doubtless "be influenced by the same vile motives with other European powers."[45] In fact, Lord Mansfield had undertaken a mysterious mission to Paris in the late summer of 1774. Although his ostensible purpose was to visit his nephew, the British ambassador at Versailles, many Englishmen assumed that he intended to negotiate some delicate political matter with the French government. Americans learned of the mission in 1775 and, because of their suspicions of the malevolently conspiratorial bent of the British ministers, saw themselves as its object.[46]

Then there was the matter of French troops in the West Indies. The first warning to the American public that France was expanding its military presence there seems to have been contained in two reports published in the *Pennsylvania Journal*, December 20, 1775: one, "that a camp for 20,000 French troops is marked out at Hispaniola, and that 7000 of them were hourly expected," and a second, that 2,500 French troops had arrived at Martinique and 1,800 at Guadaloupe, "part of a reinforcement of 10,000 men, ordered out for those islands." These reports, and similar ones, spread through America in the spring of 1776. By June it was believed that there were upwards of 30,000 French troops, accompanied by a strong fleet, in the West Indies. Actually, there were only one tenth that number.

Americans surmised that these troops were sent to strike "a severe blow," but they were not certain upon whom it would fall. Having read in the newspapers of intensive British efforts to recruit Russian and German auxiliaries, many feared that the French might have come at George III's bidding. Hardly reassuring was the king's speech at the opening of Parliament, October 27, 1775, in which he claimed that he had received "the most friendly offers of foreign assistance" and that he could unequivocally state "as well from the assurances I have received, as from the general appearance of affairs in Europe" that he could "see no probability that the measures which you may adopt, will be interrupted by disputes with any foreign power." "How is the arrival of French troops in the West-Indies, and the hostile appearance there, to be reconciled with that part of the King's speech?" wrote an anxious George Washington on January 4, 1776. Did the French "mean to act for or against America," Congress queried its agent in the West Indies a few months later?[47]

Information available in the colonies, then, seemed to give substance to Tory warnings about a partition treaty. On February 9, 1776, General Charles Lee, who five days earlier had marched into New York City to organize its defenses, wrote Robert Morris in Philadelphia: "When I consider our present situation here and at home nothing gives me so much uneasiness as the uncertainty we are in with regard to the intentions of the French in the W. Indies—it is amazing that so wise a body as the Congress should sleep over so alarming a circumstance but perhaps they have not—perhaps they have proper Instruments of Observation—if the French have a powerful Fleet as well as a large army, we may suppose they intend to attack our Islands, but if they have simply Battalions, we must conclude that there is a conclusion betwixt the two Courts—probably [Lord Mansfield?] in his expedition to Paris has enter'd into a secret engagement to let Canada slip out of our hand into theirs, these Troops may be for this purpose, but be this as it may it certainly is your business to be ascertained of their intention." Hugh Hughes of Charles Lee's quartermaster corps wrote in the same vein at the same time. Addressing John and Samuel Adams over the pseudonym "the Intelligencer," he wrote that when he considered "Ld. Mansfield's Embassy to the Court of Versailles; That Court's seconding the Views of the Court of Great Britain, in preventing our getting Arms and Ammunition, and the general Combination there is, between all the crown'd Villains, in Europe, to oppress Mankind, particularly the Neutrality observed by our Butcher, relative to the brave Corsicans, and the Arrival of such a Number of French Troops in the West Indies; I cannot, I confess, suppress my Jealousies of an Attempt being intended against Canada, in the Spring, by those Troops, and that it is already ceded to them, on the Condition of their Recovering it from us."[48]

The Whigs in Congress conceded that, although a partition was possible, it was by no means inevitable, for it would not be in France's best interests. "How is the Interest of France and Spain affected, by the dispute between B[ritain] and the C[olonies]?" wrote John Adams on March 1, 1776. "Is it the Interest of France to stand neuter, to join with B[ritain] or to join with the C[olonies]. Is it not her Interest, to dismember the B[ritish] Empire?" Or, as William Whipple wrote his brother Joseph: "Your apprehensions of Britain's forming an alliance with France, I hope is without foundation, the latter knows her own interest too well, it would be vastly more for her interest to have a Commercial alliance with the American states."[49] All the colonies needed to do to enlist France on their side, the Whigs believed, was to declare independence and offer her a commercial treaty. But they must not tarry, lest Britain win the French by default. Writing over the signature of Candidus in the *Pennsylvania Gazette* of March 6, 1776, Samuel Adams urged his colleagues to make the French ministers an offer: "A neglect to improve the openings given us . . . may inspire those statesmen with resentment, and incite them to accept overtures from our enemies, and then we may be indeed Provinces!" "Nothing, I confess, is more probable, than France's recovering Canada," if she "can have nothing to expect from us in an amiable and commercial way."[50]

Washington's success in forcing the British from Boston on March 17, 1776, was seen by the Whigs as offering additional evidence of American military prowess and of the colonies' ability to sustain themselves as independent states. For this very reason it increased fears that Britain would resort to a partition treaty and increased the urgency of beating her to the punch at the French Court. The fear of partition, in short, became a powerful motive driving Americans toward a declaration of independence. Newspapers and correspondence from April through June were full of predictions of partition and exhortations to the Whig leaders to forestall it. Letters of Patrick Henry of May 20 to Richard Henry Lee and John Adams were typical. Wrote Henry to Lee: "May not France, ignorant of the great advantages to her commerce we intend to offer, and of the permanency of that separation which is to take place, be allured by the partition you mention? To anticipate therefore the efforts of the enemy by sending instantly American Ambassadors to France, seems to me absolutely necessary." To Adams, Henry wrote "of what I think of immense importance; 'tis to anticipate the enemy at the French Court. The half of our Continent offered to France, may induce her to aid our destruction, which she certainly has the power to accomplish. I know the free trade with all the States would be more beneficial to her than any territorial possessions she might acquire. But pressed, allured, as she will be—but, above all, ignorant of the great things we mean to offer, may we not lose her?" Responding to Henry on June 3, John Adams agreed with his assessment: the "importance of an immediate application to the French court" was "clear," he averred.[51]

As sentiment for independence increased during the spring of 1776, moderates like Robert R. Livingston, Rutledge, and Wilson borrowed the Tory arguments that separation was too dangerous because it would lead to partition. Still hoping for a reconciliation with Britain in June 1776, these men argued in Congress "that France and Spain had reason to be jealous of that rising power which would one day certainly strip them of all their American possessions: that it was more likely they should form a connection with the British court, who, if they should find themselves unable otherwise to extricate themselves from their difficulties, would agree to a partition of our territories, restoring Canada to France, and the Floridas to Spain, to accomplish for themselves a recovery of these colonies." By this time the Whigs had their rejoinder down pat and replied, "That tho' France and Spain may be jealous of our rising power, they must think it will be much more formidable with the addition of Great Britain; and will therefore see it their interest to prevent a coalition."[52] There would, therefore, be no partition, if Congress hastened to declare independence and approach the Bourbons.

How was the approach to France to be managed? Interested though she was in helping America, might she not take advantage of the new nation's needs to extort exorbitant concessions from her? In the guise of a helper might she not become a master? Ever fearful of France, Whigs worried about this question. Tories tried to exaggerate their apprehensions by striking up the anti-French propaganda of earlier colonial wars. William Smith, writing as Cato in the *Pennsylvania Gazette*, March 27, 1776, went far beyond Galloway's anti-French screeds of a year earlier. Were the Whigs really proposing that "both branches of the Bourbon Family, so long the terror of Protestants and Freemen, should now join as their protectors"? Were Protestant America's ancient fears now to be dismissed as "prejudice"? Must the colonists divest themselves "of every opinion in which we have been educated . . . and throw down what our fathers and we have been building up for ages"? It would be superlative folly to negotiate with France, which was so little to be trusted that "Gallican Fides, or French Faith, is become as proverbial now, as Punica Fides, or Carthaginian Faith, of old." "Bloody massacres, the revocation of sacred edicts, and the most unrelenting persecutions," continued Smith, "have certainly taught American protestants . . . what sort of faith we are to expect from Popish Princes." Any kind of diplomatic relations with Versailles would, in Smith's view, force America, sooner or later, to "submit to the absolute dominion of France." Inglis took the same line, insisting that the colonies could procure assistance from France only if she "were sure of some extraordinary advantage by it, in having the colonies under her immediate jurisdiction."[53]

Tory fear-mongering caused Whig leaders constantly to reassure their followers, who like Landon Carter apprehended "danger from our being aided by despotic States," that they were properly wary of France and Spain. "Great Care is certainly to be taken by the Colonies in forming such an Alliance," Elbridge Gerry wrote a friend on June 11, 1776; never would the colonies "exchange British for French tyranny," John Adams assured James Warren on April 16, 1776. The assistance to be requested from the Bourbons would not, in any case, give them a handle to oppress America. "Will the help we desire," wrote Richard Henry Lee to Landon Carter on June 2, 1776, "put it, by any means in the power of France to hurt us tho she were so inclined. Supplies of Military Stores and Soldiers Clothing, ships of war to cover our Trade and open our Ports, which would be an external assistance altogether, could never endanger our freedom by putting it in the power of our Ally to Master us." John Adams's views were similar. To those who feared that "France will take Advantage of us . . . and demand severe Terms of Us," he answered that America's military power was so great that she did not need the protection of French armies. Boasting about "young Hercules" on April 16, 1776, he asserted that Britain and France together would "have good luck to get" dominion over America. He was not, therefore, for "soliciting any political Connection, or military assistance or indeed naval from France. I wish for nothing," he wrote John Winthrop on June 23, "but Commerce, a mere marine treaty with them."[54] In this kind of relationship, how could France oppress America?

In response to Richard Henry Lee's motion of June 7, proposing that the colonies declare independence, establish a confederation, and "take the most effectual means for forming alliances," Congress on June 11 moved the appointment of a committee to prepare a plan of treaties to be offered to foreign nations and the next day named five members: John Adams, Benjamin Franklin, John Dickinson, Benjamin Harrison, and Robert Morris. The intellectual atmosphere in which the committee worked and the problems that most concerned it can be grasped by focusing on the July 1 debate over independence, a debate that paid considerable attention to the foreign-policy implications of independence and summarized much of the preceding months' discussion of the problem. John Adams was the principal Whig spokesman in the debate, in which he solidified his claim to the title "the Atlas of Independence." Adams's speech does not survive. According to his later account of it he said nothing new, nothing that had not been repeated several times before.[55] He must, therefore, have stressed the power of America, the power of Britain which it sustained, and the interest of France in separating the two countries lest their combined might reduce her to an international cypher.

Presenting the case against independence and for reconciliation with Britain was John Dickinson, notes of whose speech do survive.[56] Dickinson addressed himself to the fear that Britain would partition the colonies with France and Spain if she could not conquer America. He agreed with Adams and others of his adversaries that America could prevent a partition by offering France a commercial treaty: "Gentlemen say the Trade of all America is more valuable to France than Canada. I grant it." But Dickinson expected France to drive a hard bargain in commercial negotiations with America. He thought it foolish, therefore, to declare independence forthwith, because from such a step America could not recede and, as moderates like Rutledge had argued earlier, the colonies would be "placing ourselves in the Power of those with whom we mean to treat." Far better, it appeared to Dickinson and his supporters, to hold a declaration of independence in abeyance and to treat with France "before hand and settle the terms of any future alliance."[57] The moderate strategy was, in other words, to use a declaration of independence as a bargaining counter to extract reasonable terms from France. As it was, Dickinson feared that France would "intimidate Us into a most disadvantageous Grant of our Trade." If France obtained control over American trade, Britain, deprived of the source of her power, would be ruined. Who, then, would protect America from France? Who would be the guarantor of the nation's security? "Suppose we shall ruin her," said an anxious Dickinson. "France must rise on her Ruins. Her Ambition. Her Religion. Our Danger from thence. We shall weep at our victories."

The principal concern in drawing the plan of treaties was national security in a brutal, amoral world. If the treaty plan were not correctly calculated, a concert of nations might fall like brigands on America and partition her. Or, if this danger were avoided, France, perhaps Spain, and who could predict what other European predator, might attempt to subjugate the country as soon as the ruin of Britain was confirmed. The task of drafting the plan of treaties fell to John Adams, who was recognized, even by opponents, as one of Congress's keenest students of foreign affairs—James Duane, no friend of Adams, told him in the fall of 1775, "We all agree that you have more fully considered and better digested the subject of foreign connections than any man we have ever heard speak on the subject."[58] Adams's draft was reported to Congress on July 18, 1776. It was read that day and on July 20 eighty copies were printed for the members' perusal. Precedence was given, however, to consideration of the articles of confederation, which were, William Williams wrote a friend on August 12, the "Standing Dish of Congress." On August 19 Rutledge complained that "we have not yet touched the treaty—and Independence has been declared upwards of six weeks!"[59] Three days later Congress resolved itself into a committee of the whole to consider the treaty. On August 27 the treaty was considered again and congressmen were able to report that it "has passed in the Committee of the whole."[60] The dispatch with which the treaty plan passed, compared with the prolonged dissension over the articles of confederation, shows that there was a consensus in Congress on foreign affairs and that Adams expressed it in his draft. At the committee of the whole's direction, some alterations were made in the Model Treaty, as it is often called, which did not, however, significantly change its substance. The new version was approved by Congress on September 17.

The Model Treaty's goal was simple: to dissolve the British monopoly of American commerce and to invite all nations, Great Britain not excepted, to trade with the United States on equal terms. The purpose of the treaty plan was to provide for American security by using American commerce to maintain the European balance of power. On March 20, 1783, Adams informed James Warren of the intellectual context from which the Model Treaty emerged:

> Gentlemen can never too often [be] requested to recollect the Debates in Congress in the Years 1775 and 1776, when the Treaty with France was first in Con-

templation. The Nature of those Connections, which
ought to be formed between America and Europe, will
never be better understood than they were at that time.
It was then said, there is a Ballance of Power in Europe.
Nature has formed it. Practice and Habit have confirmed it, and it must exist forever. It may be disturbed
for a time, by the accidental Removal of a Weight from
one Scale to the other; but there will be a continual
Effort to restore the Equilibrium. . . . if We give exclusive priviledges in Trade, or form perpetual Alliances
offensive and defensive with the Powers in one Scale,
we infallibly make enemies of those in the other . . .
Congress adopted these Principles and this System
in its purity.[61]

Adams and his colleagues knew the consequences of denying
"exclusive privileges in Trade" to France, of putting Britain and
her on an equal footing in American trade: Britain would obtain
the lion's share of it. Thomas Paine pointed this out as early as
February 14, 1776, in an appendix to *Common Sense*: "It is the
commerce and not the conquest of America, by which England
is to be benefited, and that would in a great measure continue,
were the countries as independent of each other as France and
Spain: because in many articles, neither can go to a better mar-
ket." Franklin made the same observation in a letter to Lord
Howe of July 20, 1776—with an equal trade with an independent America, Britain, the Doctor asserted, "might recover a
great Share of our Regard and the greatest part of our growing
Commerce, with all the Advantage of that additional Strength
to be derived from a Friendship with us." And Rutledge repeated this point to Howe at the Staten Island conference of
September 11, 1776.[62] Like Paine, Adams perceived that Britain
would enjoy a competitive advantage in American commerce—
she could sell her commodities "to them [the Americans]
cheaper, and give them a better price for theirs than any other
nation." As a result, he foresaw that Britain would obtain "more

of American Trade . . . than France" and would derive from it "more support" for her navy than the French would. She would, he was convinced, "recover . . . much of her Commerce, and perhaps equal Consideration and Profit and Power from [the Americans] as ever"; she would "find as much real advantage from them, and more too than [she] ever did."[63]

Consequently, would a grateful Britain not befriend America again? By no means, Adams believed. The friendship of Britain, he was certain, was gone forever. On July 1, 1776, he predicted that war between Britain and America "would terminate in an incurable animosity between the two Countries." Britain would be America's "natural Enemy for the future," who "would clean the wooden shoes of the French upon Condition that they would permit them to wreak their Vengeance on us." The British "hate us, universally, from the throne to the footstool," he wrote John Jay on August 13, 1782, "and would annihilate us, if in their power." Why, then, draw a treaty to sustain Britain's strength? Because Adams believed that it was in the United States' interest to do so. The United States, he contended, "ought with the utmost Firmness to Resist every thought of giving to France any unequal advantage in our Trade even over England, for it never could be our Interest to ruin England, or annihilate their maritime Power, if we could possibly save our Liberty and independence without it." "In the years 1775 and 1776," Adams recalled later, he "laid it down as a first principle that . . . above all . . . it could never be our interest to ruin Great Britain, or injure or weaken her any further than should be necessary to our independence." Why? Because "neither England nor America could depend upon the Moderation of such absolute Monarchies and such ambitious Nations" as France and Spain, because, as Benjamin Rush recalled Adams saying in 1776, "the time might come when we should be obliged to call upon Britain to defend us against France."[64]

The Model Treaty was conceived to benefit France, too. Giving France equal access to American trade would, Adams assumed, extend her "navigation and Trade, augment her resources of naval Power . . . and place her on a more equal footing with England." But no one expected the Model Treaty to raise France to an equality of power with Britain. As Adams wrote in 1780, although France "should profit by American commerce, she [Britain] and her friends would profit more. The balance will be preserved, and she will have nothing to fear."[65] Neither would the United States have reason to fear, for the balance that the Model Treaty was designed to create would leave Britain and France strong enough to prevent each other from destroying American independence, which each would do, Americans believed, if they could.

Adams and his colleagues did not place sole reliance on the operations of the balance of power to protect them. They firmly believed in what we today would call the doctrine of deterrence; that is, they believed that in the predatory world they inhabited the possession of power and the willingness to use it were guarantors of peace. In other words, they subscribed to the ancient maxim: "si velis pacem, para bellum"—if you want peace, prepare for war. This, John Adams claimed in 1808, had been his system throughout his life. It had been the system of his compatriots, too. Jefferson: "Whatever enables us to go to war, secures our peace"; "Weakness provokes insult and injury, while a condition to punish it prevents it." Washington: "If we desire to secure peace . . . it must be known that we are at all times ready for War"; "To be prepared for War is the most effectual means of preserving peace." Franklin: "The Way to secure Peace is to be prepared for War." Jay: "We should remember that to be constantly prepared for war is the only way to have peace." Henry: "A preparation for Warr is necessary to obtain peace." Marshall: "If we be prepared to defend ourselves, there will be little inducement to attack." Gadsden: "The only way to prevent the sword from being used is to have it ready." And Richard Henry Lee: "Our leaders [should] engrave upon their minds the wisdom of the inscription upon the arsenal of Berne in Switzerland—'that people happy are, who, during peace, are preparing the necessary stores for war.' "[66]

American leaders were not power hungry—at least not until Hamilton's military ambitions ran amok in the late 1790s. They believed that an impressive military establishment was easily within young Hercules' reach. Adams, for example, wrote to Jay in 1785 that if British commercial warfare forced the United States to adopt a navigation act in retaliation, America could, in ten years, have the third navy in the world. But why, he asked, would Britain force us "to try experiments against our own inclinations?"[67] He and his colleagues did not want a surfeit of military power, because they feared it would be fatal to the republican government they wished so desperately to maintain. The power they wanted was modest: adequate military supplies, well-disciplined militias in each state, and a middling naval force. This power, coupled with America's vast land mass and booming population, would, they felt, deter any potential enemy, whom the operation of the balance of power failed to restrain.

If eighteenth-century European diplomacy was, as Felix Gilbert claimed, "entirely dominated by the concept of power,"[68] the same can be said of the foreign policy of Revolutionary America, as formulated by John Adams and his colleagues. That the conventional European doctrines of the balance of power and of the interest of states should have dominated their thinking is not surprising. These were the modes of analysis on which they, as citizens of the British Empire, had been born and raised. When the time came to craft a foreign policy for the new American nation, they quite naturally employed them.

CHAPTER 2

FRANCE, 1778-1779

Although Adams's grasp of foreign affairs impressed his friends and political associates and made him a prime candidate, in their eyes, to represent the United States abroad, he did not, in 1776, regard himself as a potential diplomat. His forte, he believed, was domestic polity. "Every Colony," he wrote William Cushing on June 9, "must be induced to institute a perfect Government. All the Colonies must confederate together, in some Solemn Compact." Independence must be declared and the treaty plan drafted. "When these Things shall be once well finished, or in a Way of being so, I shall think that I have answered the End of my Creation." To Mercy Otis Warren, who in the spring of 1776 expected that Adams would soon be writing her about "noble and Royal Characters," he replied on April 16 with a recitation of his deficiencies for diplomacy. "Your Correspondent has neither Principles, nor Address, nor Abilities, for such Scenes. And others are as Sensible of it, I assure you as he is. They must be Persons of more Complaisance and Ductility of Temper as well as better Accomplishments for such great Things." In the fall of 1776 Adams rebuffed Elbridge Gerry's attempt to nominate him as one of the United States' commissioners to France. "R. H. Lee told me," Gerry wrote later, "You had informed him, that You would not accept the appointment if made." On November 7, 1777, after three years of grueling service in Congress, Adams left Philadelphia and returned to Massachusetts to repair his health and finances. Three weeks later Congress elected him to replace Silas Deane as one of its commissioners at the Court of Louis XVI. Adams was flabbergasted when he received the news; he later confided to a correspondent that "he had as many thoughts of a Voyage to the Moon as to France." But after wrestling with his conscience, he decided to accept the trust and on February 13, 1778, departed for Europe aboard the American frigate *Boston*. After running a gauntlet of North Atlantic storms and British warships, he arrived safely at Bordeaux on April 1, 1778.[1]

For the next ten years, with a break of a few months in 1779, Adams represented the United States at various European courts. He never deviated from his balance of power thinking, but conceptualizing foreign policy yielded precedence in Europe to personal interaction with other diplomats—to what Adams liked to call his "negotiations"—and in these he was governed by another set of attitudes—by no means inconsistent, as will be later shown, with his balance of power thinking—which developed during the Revolutionary struggle with Britain, specifically, by the suspicion, almost the expectation, that a malign conspiracy was fixing its sights on virtuous Americans with the intention of oppressing them. In a series of books on the ideological origins of the American Revolution, Bernard Bailyn has argued that Americans were "propelled" into revolution by the pervasive fear of a British ministerial conspiracy to enslave them.[2] Adams was an early and ardent believer in the existence of a ministerial conspiracy: "There seems to be a direct and formal design on foot to enslave all America," he wrote in 1765.[3] The conspiracy theory gained potency from a conviction that grew in America in the 1760s that suspicion itself was a positive good. Revolutionary Americans used the term jealousy to mean suspicion and, unlike their twentieth-century descendents, carefully distinguished jealousy from envy, which, then as now, meant resentment of a rival's success.[4] "A perpetual jealously respecting liberty," asserted John Dickinson in his authoritative *Letters from a Farmer in Pennsylvania* (1768), "is absolutely requisite in all free states."[5] Jealousy was extolled as a "moral" and "political virtue" from one end of the country to another and it was legitimitized in the independent United States by receiving the imprimatur of republicanism, the designation which, after 1776, made all things acceptable.[6]

As with the conspiracy theory, Adams was an early apostle of jealousy, commending a "jealous Watchful Spirit"[7] in 1765 and practicing what he preached throughout the conflict with Britain. Alexander Hamilton was repelled by Adams's suspiciousness during his presidency. He possessed "a jealousy capable of discoloring every object," wrote the New Yorker, an assessment in which Mercy Otis Warren concurred a few years later when she claimed that Adams's mind was "replete with jealousy." But what Hamilton and Warren took to be a surfeit of suspicion in Adams was merely a continuation of, or, according to one observer, a moderation of, his jealousy during the Revolutionary years. Adams, wrote Theodore Sedgwick in 1788, "was formerly infinitely more democratical than at present and possessing that jealousy which always accompanies such a character was averse to repose . . . unlimited confidence" in anyone.[8]

Jealousy-suspicion flourished, indeed luxuriated, in Revolutionary America. "Jealousy was prevalent in Republicks," observed Silas Deane in December 1777, and "its greatest degree was now excited in America."[9] Fused with the fear of conspiracy, it quickened that fear to such an extent that the most innocuous political maneuvers were often interpreted as steps in a plot to persecute the innocent. The Revolutionary mentality, therefore, strikes modern scholars conversant with the literature of psychopathology as paranoiac. "The era of the American Revolution," it is asserted, "was a period of political paranoia."[10] "The insurgent whig ideology had a frenzied even paranoid cast to it," writes one scholar; another hears it sounding "a paranoiac note." A third stresses its "paranoiac obsession with a diabolical

Crown conspiracy."[11] Some scholars have concluded that the ideology's pathological complexion rubbed off on those who espoused it—the Revolutionary statesmen. "It is not uncommon," writes an essayist in 1976, "for whig publicists and leaders to be viewed as paranoid."[12] John Adams was the first to admit that he was frequently buffeted by emotional turbulence: "There have been many times in my life," he wrote, "when I have been so agitated in my own mind as to have no consideration at all of the light in which my words, actions, and even writings would be considered by others."[13] The most perceptive of Adams's recent biographers has, in fact, contended that he suffered no less than three nervous breakdowns between 1771 and 1783.[14] Therefore, it is not surprising that he has attracted the attention of those seeking pathological strains in Revolutionary statesmen and that he has received his share of diagnoses as paranoid.[15] It is not, however, the intention of this study to put Adams on the couch to confirm or refute the presence of a pathological component in his psyche. The term paranoid, when applied to him, will be used as Bailyn uses it in his magisterial studies[16]—simply as a descriptive phrase to convey the intensity of the suspiciousness and of the fears of malevolent conspiracy which infused the Revolutionary mentality and which appeared, with unusual force, in Adams's conduct as a diplomat.

Apprehensions about European nations conspiring to partition America were, of course, one product of the suspicious and fearful Revolutionary mind. Another was the conclusion Adams reached after some months' exposure to French diplomacy in Paris that the Court of Louis XVI was conspiring to dominate the United States, a duplication, in fact, of his earlier suspicion that Britain was conspiring to enslave America. When he arrived in Paris on April 1, 1778, Adams's suspicions were first aroused, however, by his own colleagues. The initial phase of his diplomatic career was, therefore, a story of interpersonal relations, dominated not only by fear and suspicion but also by anger, mortification, envy, and egotism, practically the whole gamut of the tempestuous passions. This period differs conspicuously from the preceding years in which he was the dominant figure in formulating American foreign policy. From 1774 to 1776 Adams, insofar as he was concerned with foreign affairs, appears as a powerful intellect in full control of the intellectual universe of international relations. But from 1778 onward he often seems to be the sport of passions. The mastery of 1774–1776 yields, after 1778, to periods of drift; we see a man bobbing along on powerful emotional currents, which often threaten to wreck him but which finally bring him to a safe, if not altogether happy, haven.

Even before alighting from the *Boston* at Bordeaux, Adams learned that the American commissioners at Versailles—Franklin, Deane, and Lee—had on February 6, 1778, signed treaties of alliance and commerce with Louis XVI. The objective of his mission, to assist in the negotiation of these treaties, had thus been accomplished before he set foot on French soil. His hopes of cutting a figure in Europe having been dashed at its doorstep, he was tempted to take the first ship home. On April 16 a British agent reported from Paris that "J. Adams is arrived very disappointed to find everything concluded, talks of returning."[17]

Talk of returning he might, for the United States had as little need of three ministers at Paris as of three commanders-in-chief of its armies. Had Adams been so inclined, he could have relaxed and enjoyed the social and intellectual stimulation of the French capital. But he could not abide self-indulgence and desperately needed to be doing something useful. Therefore, he made himself the custodian of the commission's papers, served as its paymaster, and became its penman as well, doing the work other men would have relegated to their clerks. He studied French "like a school Boy." After a short time he began to decline social invitations. He even chose to do without a carriage. "I am," he boasted to his wife, "the first public Minister that ever lived without a Carriage."[18]

John Adams

In trying so earnestly to serve his country, Adams resembled nothing so much as a dog chasing its tail. And he knew it, because on July 26, 1778, he informed James Lovell that he was "fully persuaded" that the public's interests were "not at all concerned in my Residence here."[19] But he kept trying to justify his presence in France with diligent attention to the commission's business; nothing less would allow him to keep peace with himself.

Another disappointment for Adams was the discovery that the American community in France was riven with disputes. "I never heard in my Life, of any Misunderstanding among any of the Commissioners, that I can recollect, untill my Arrival at Bordeaux. I had not been on shore an hour before I learn'd it," he wrote in September 1779.[20] Arrayed against each other were Franklin, Deane, Dr. Edward Bancroft, and their followers on one side and Arthur Lee, William Lee, Ralph Izard, and their supporters on the other. Americans and Frenchmen had taken sides in the quarrel and had magnified the differences to such a degree that they had become a matter of public notoriety throughout France.

Adams had served in the Continental Congress with Franklin and Deane and admired them both. With Franklin, Adams enjoyed "that kind of Friendship, which is commonly felt between two members of the same public Assembly . . . who always agreed in their Opinions and Sentiments of public affairs."[21] Deane had impressed Adams so much that he wrote a glowing testimonial for him on November 5, 1775: "There is scarcely a more active, industrious, enterprising and capable Man, than Mr. Deane . . . Men of such great daring active Spirits are much Wanted."[22] Arthur Lee had spent the pre-independence years in London where he served as Massachusetts Bay's auxiliary agent. Though Adams was a close ally in Congress of Arthur's brothers Richard Henry and Francis Lightfoot Lee, he had never met Arthur, knowing him only through his correspondence with Massachusetts political leaders, correspondence that, in his opinion, breathed the "most inflexible attachment and the most ardent zeal in the cause of his country."[23]

Temperamentally, Adams was closer to Arthur Lee than to Franklin, who was affecting in Paris the urbanity and detachment of the venerable philosopher, or to Deane, whose head was usually swimming with commercial ventures. Like Adams, Lee was a man of passion—his temper "would raise Quarrels in the Elisian Field," Adams once wrote[24]—and of jealousy. According to William Carmichael, Lee was "excessively jealous and suspicious," a charge that, when repeated to Adams by an official of the French Foreign Ministry, he agreed was correct.[25] Lee, in fact, believed that there could never be too much jealousy, that it was "a spirit we ought to respect, even in its excesses." Lee's friends defended his hypersuspiciousness as a commendable example of "Republican Jealousy." Enemies like Deane believed that his "head was affected," that his "jealous disposition" made him the victim of delusions, led him to "apprehend designs injurious to him in every one he dealt with." A former British patron, Lord Shelburne, considered him "a Madman whenever his Passions are inflamed."[26] Modern writers have called him, as they have called Adams, "paranoid."[27] Although Adams thought Lee's suspicions were frequently exaggerated and often found him abrasive, he recognized him as a kindred spirit and treated him with respect. Being well disposed, then, to Franklin, Deane, and Lee, Adams found it easy, during the first months of his mission, to adopt a policy of benevolent neutrality toward them, to cut through the clouds of calumnies surrounding them, and to pronounce them ''honest Men, and devoted friends to their Country."[28]

By deed as well as by word Adams hoped to calm the passions and conciliate the dispositions of his colleagues. Izard's fulminations against Franklin, for example, had so overcome the Doctor's philosophy that he refused to invite him to social events at the American "embassy." Adams, therefore, invited both men to dinner in hopes of promoting a reconciliation. But after this and other efforts failed, he recognized that the quarrels among his countrymen had become too inveterate to compose and ceased his attempts at peacemaking.[29]

The final disagreeable surprise awaiting Adams was one that he did not attempt—indeed did not know how—to remedy. He had not been in Paris long before he learned that Deane, who departed just before he arrived, had complained of "ill treatment" in being recalled by Congress. The construction that Adams put upon Deane's complaints was not that, upon returning to America, he would seek justice from those who had recalled him; rather, Adams feared that Deane would retaliate against him personally, even though he was in Massachusetts, hundreds of miles from Congress, when the decision to replace Deane was made. "How soon attempts may be made to displace me I know not," Adams wrote James Lovell on July 26, 1778, "but one thing I beg of my Friends, and one only that if any Attempt of that kind should be made, they would give me up."[30]

During the same month Bancroft showed Adams a letter from Deane's brother and business partner, Barnabas, in which John Hancock was mentioned "as being extremly sorry Mr. D. was recalled—that Congress did not do it—that it was done after the Members were withdrawn and Congress very thin." Adams's interpretation of this letter was that Hancock was maligning *him*, accusing *him* of contriving Deane's demise for his own benefit. "The whole Letter," he commented, "was the Effect of a miserable Jealousy and Envy of me. I felt no little Indignation, at the ill Will, which had instigated this Persecution against me across the Atlantic."[31]

In September Adams saw, in a London evening newspaper, what purported to be an intercepted letter to Silas Deane from another brother, Simeon, which stated "that the two Adams are strongly against you," that he, Simeon, could not predict "to what lengths the two A's intend to push their 'Factions.' " To which accusations Adams responded: "I never in my Life knew a Man displaced from a Trust, but he and his Friends were angry with his successor. I therefore expected this, and am not disappointed."[32]

Meanwhile, on September 14, 1778, Congress put its affairs in France on a more sensible footing by abolishing the three-member commission and appointing Benjamin Franklin sole minister to the court to Louis XVI. Word of Franklin's appointment reached Adams at the end of November, not from Congress but from a private letter of Deane to Franklin, September 15, whose contents were noised around Paris. Adams, it was rumored, would be sent to Vienna or recalled, both "disagreeable" prospects for him.[33]

Weeks passed in "total Suspense and Uncertainty," as Adams awaited official word of his fate.[34] It came on February 12, 1779, in dispatches from Congress, carried by Lafayette's aide-de-camp. Deane's report was confirmed. The commission was dissolved and Franklin was appointed sole minister to France. Lee retained his old post as commissioner to Spain. And Adams? Nothing for Adams. No reassignment, not even a letter of recall. Adams was hurt, humiliated, angry. "The Scaffold is cutt away," he wrote his wife on February 28, "and I am left kicking and sprawling in the Mire. . . . It is hardly a state of Disgrace that I am in but rather of total Neglect and Contempt. . . . If I had committed any Crime which deserved to hang me up in a Gibet in the Face of all Europe, I ought to have been told what it is."[35]

When the reports about the alteration in the American commission began circulating in Paris at the end of November 1778, Adams speculated that conspirators had produced the change, that he had been the victim of the intrigues of a coterie of "fine gentlemen"—Deane, Hancock, and their mercantile associates. "I expect," he wrote his wife on December 3, "by some Letters I have seen from the Weathersfield Family [Deane's home was Wethersfield, Connecticut], that a certain fine Gentleman will join another fine Gentleman, and these some other fine Gentlemen, to obtain some Arrangement that shall dishonnour me.

And by Hints that are given out here, I should not wonder if I shall be recalled, or sent to Vienna which would be worse."[36]

But was Deane capable of conspiring to dishonor him? In December 1778 Adams was struggling to keep an open mind on the question. His suspicions of Deane, it is true, were deepening. Such a man needed "always to be carefully watched and controlled," he wrote James Warren on December 5.[37] Hardly reassuring, moreover, were the accusations against Arthur Lee which had been coming from Deane's friends; Lee, the French ministry was being told, was betraying allied secrets to the British, a "cruel Calumny" in Adams's view, and an indication, apparently, that no man's reputation was safe in the poisonous atmosphere of the American community in Paris. Adams, however, was reluctant to ascribe these insinuations directly to Deane.[38] But there were limits to his forbearance toward his fellow New Englander and these were breached by the appearance in Europe early in 1779 of Deane's "Address to the Free and Virtuous Citizens of America."

Published in the *Pennsylvania Packet* on December 5, the "Address" was reprinted in London in the January 26–28 issue of the *St. James Chronicle* and in Paris in the February 2 issue of the *Courier de l'Europe*, where Adams read it. The "Address" was a broadside against the Lee family, charging its members with committing treason against the United States in both Europe and America. Adams was infuriated. "One of the most wicked and abominable Productions that ever sprung from an Human Heart," he declared. Deane was nothing less than "a wild boar, that ought to be hunted down for the Benefit of Mankind," a miscreant who ought to be given up to "Satan to be buffeted."[39] And on and on Adams raged.

The intemperance of his response to the "Address" was produced by the belief that it demonstrated that Deane had, in fact, contrived to remove him from the embassy to France. The Adamses and Lees had collaborated in the struggle for independence so closely that some historians have suggested, only half facetiously, that the Revolution was a product of a temporary alliance between the two families. Adams, therefore, took the assault against the Lees personally. If the Lee family grew "unpopular among their fellow Citizens," he did not know "what Family or what Person, will stand the Test."[40] In light of the "Accusation against Mr. L" he would not, he wrote his wife on February 20, "be at all surprised" to see "an Accusation against me for something or other."[41] That his name was not mentioned in the "Address" did not reassure him.

With "proof" now at hand that Deane and his cronies were out to get him, Adams began planning countermeasures. "I will not always see the Honour and Interest of my Country intrigued away and her most solid Characters immolated at the Shrine of Molock and be silent," he wrote Edmund Jenings in June.[42] After returning to America in August, Adams picked up the refrain, lamenting to James Lovell on September 10, that "so many Characters as meritorious as any that ever served this Continent, should be immolated not to Divinities but to a Gang of Peddlers." Adams was not intimidated by the peddlers, however, for he informed Lovell, "I don't dread . . . for myself nor much for the publick, taking Mr. D[eane] in his own Way but I should go a little deeper than Mr. Paine did";[43] this meant that Adams was not reluctant to attack Deane in the newspapers (as Deane had attacked the Lees in his "Address") and that he believed he could draw a more damaging indictment against him than could Thomas Paine, who, stepping forward as an avenger of the Lees, had previously assailed Deane in the public prints.

But vindication in the newspapers was not enough for Adams. On September 10 he wrote Congress, stating "a Claim upon the Justice of my Country, that my Reputation may not be permitted to be stained unless I deserve it." Explaining that he was absent when Deane was recalled, he asked for "Copies of those Complaints and Evidences, and the Names of my Accusers and Witnesses against me, that I may take such Measures as may be in my Power to justify myself before Congress."[44]

Congress did not supply Adams with the names of his accusers and adverse witnesses because there were none; they existed only in his imagination, which is to say, that the conviction which we have been watching develop in Adams's mind that he had been "immolated" by a confederacy of malefactors was something approximating a delusion of persecution.[45] Only one link in the chain of "evidence" which convinced him that Deane and his associates had sacrificed him was a legitimate indication of hostility toward him—the September 1778 intercepted letter from Simeon to Silas Deane—and Adams was not without suspicions that it had been forged. All other "evidence" consisted of statements which did not, on their face, concern Adams at all— Deane's complaining of "ill treatment" in being recalled, Hancock's claiming that Congress had not recalled Deane, Deane's attacking the Lees—but from which Adams inferred enmity toward himself.

Once the conviction of Deane's evil doing took root in Adams's mind, it could not be extirpated. Both Samuel Adams and James Lovell tried to reassure him. In letters that accompanied the official announcement of the dissolution of the American commission, Lovell declared, "Your Honor and Happiness are dear to me and to many others. The Delay of Republican Assemblies is the only thing against you. Your Character is esteemed"; Samuel Adams wrote in the same strain, telling his cousin, "Congress entertain great Expectation from your Services." But these letters were simply swept aside as Adams's suspicions of Deane mounted. Lovell continued to try to put him at ease. On June 13 he wrote that there appeared to be "no Plot concealed under the Professions in your Favor which have fallen from Men lately whose general Conduct is of a Kind to make me cry times Danaos vel dona ferentes." And on August 20 he informed Adams, "You have not an Enemy amongst us." As secretary of Congress's Committee of Foreign Affairs and an Argus-eyed defender of Adams's interests, Lovell should have been able to dispel his apprehensions about Deane. But Adams dismissed his testimony out of hand, advising him on September 10, "to reconsider your Opinions concerning my Friends and Enemies in Congress."[46] His suspicions about Deane had reached the stage where they would brook no contradiction, however authoritative.

The humiliation of being discharged from diplomatic service produced suspicions, not only about Deane but about Franklin as well. The dissolution of the commission to France meant more than Adams's abasement; it also meant Franklin's elevation. That Adams was envious of Franklin's success in becoming sole minister to France is certain. One need not document it by anecdotes like that of Dr. James Smith, who alleged that at a dinner party given by Madame Bertin "the portrait of Franklin was introduced on the stage . . . an universal burst of applause ensued, which wounded the feelings of Adams to such a degree, that he feigned sickness and left the performance."[47] One need not even rely on the observations of Turgot, a frequent visitor at Passy, who noted, on March 18, that Adams was "cankered with excessive envy" of Franklin.[48] One need only look at Adams's writings.

Until reports of Franklin's elevation began circulating in Paris at the end of November 1778, Adams treated the Doctor with unfailing kindness. This cannot have been easy, for Adams was growing increasingly irritated by the adulation Parisians were showering on Franklin, while he himself was being treated as a "perfect Cypher."[49] For Adams, insignificance was "as severe a pain as the gout or the stone" and, therefore, he complained to Luzerne, the French minister-designate with whom he sailed to America in the summer of 1779, how he had "seen . . . with displeasure the attention which the Parisians have lavished on M. Franklin, while he was hardly known at all."[50] Adams, however, suppressed his resentment of Franklin until word got out that he would be sole minister at Versailles. Then the disparagement of envy began to fill Adams's letters. Was Franklin's reputation in Paris unprecedented? It was a fraud, produced by puffery. "A man must be his own Trumpeter," Adams wrote James Warren on December 2, 1778; "He must ostentatiously publish to the World his own Writings with his Name, and must write even some Panegyrics on them, he must get his Picture drawn, his Statue made, and must hire all the Artists in his Turn, to set about Works to spread his Name, make the Mob stare and gape, and perpetuate his Fame. I would undertake, if I could bring my Feelings to bear it, to become one of the most trumpeted, admired, courted, worship'd Idols in the whole World in four or five Years."[51] Was Franklin able to manage as sole minister? Very doubtful. His mind, Adams wrote Samuel Adams on December 5, was "in such a constant State of Dissipation that if he is left here alone, the public Business will suffer in a degree beyond description." Congress must "take out of his hands the public Treasury, and the Direction of the Frigates and continental Vessells that are sent here, and all Commercial affairs"; otherwise, "France and America will both have reason to repent it."[52] After the confirmation of Franklin's appointment arrived in Paris on February 12, Adams became more strident, criticizing the Doctor's "Indolence," "Dissipation," and "Indiscretion," warning that if "mercantile and maritime matters and the Disposition of all Money but his own Salary is not taken from the Minister, America will be ruined in Reputation as well as Credit," and asserting that he was "not a sufficient Statesman for all the Business he is in. He knows too little of American Affairs and of the Politicks of Europe and takes too little Pains to inform himself of either."[53] The evidence is clear; Adams was consumed with an envy of Franklin, which he never overcame.[54]

Adams was envious of Franklin because he considered himself his competitor for the position of minister to France. How could a colonial lawyer, with a provincial reputation only, regard himself as a competitor with one of the most famous men of the age? The answer was Adams's celebrated vanity. "Vanity," he wrote at age twenty-one, "is my cardinal Vice and cardinal Folly"[55] and neither friends nor enemies ever disputed this point with him. Sometimes Adams's vanity was no more than the boasting of an

unguarded moment; as, for example, when he informed his wife
on April 11, 1783, that he had performed such services as "were
never rendered by any other Minister in Europe."[56] At other
times, however, his self-esteem soared to the stratosphere. Those
effusive Parisians who called him "le Washington de la Négotiation" were only stating an obvious fact.[57] So was the Abbé Raynal when he said that "John Adams est un des plus grandes
Hommes D'Etat de cette Siècle."[58] And so, for that matter, was
James Otis, when he declared, "John Adams would one day be
the greatest man in North America."[59] As Adams saw it,
Thomas Jefferson was not the principal figure in the declaration
of American Independence. He was, for it was he who had proposed the impeachment of Massachusetts Chief Justice Andrew
Oliver in February 1774. Was the relationship between the two
events obscure? Not to Adams—he "was the author of the impeachment, and consequently the author of independence."
The convention that met in Philadelphia in 1787 was not the
principal architect of the United States Constitution. John
Adams was—his *Defense of the Constitutions of Government of
the United States*, written in London the same year, had produced it. Adams's old friend Mercy Warren caustically, but accurately, described the role Adams conceived that he had played
in American public affairs: "His writings suppressed rebellion
[Shays'], quelled the insurgents, established the State and Federal Constitutions, and gave the United States all the liberty, republicanism, and independence they enjoy . . . nothing had
been done, nothing could be done, neither in Europe nor America, without his sketching and drafting the business, from the
first opposition to British measures in 1764 to signing the treaty
of peace with England in the year 1783."[60] So what, then, if
Benjamin Franklin was, by Adams's own admission, more re-
nowned than "Leibnits or Newton, Frederick or Voltaire?"[61] Did
one of the "greatest statesmen of the century" not have the right
to compete with him for the post at Versailles and the excuse to
be envious, if he failed to receive it?

Adams's vanity extended to his private as well as his public life. Of nothing was he prouder, nothing did he estimate more highly, than his moral character. He simply believed that he was the incarnation of Moral Good. I will not, he wrote his wife on July 1, 1774, "see Blockheads . . . elevated above me . . . nor shall Knavery . . . get the better of Honesty, nor Ignorance of Knowledge, nor Folly of Wisdom, nor Vice of Virtue." His "Character," he wrote some years later, was "fortified with a Shield of Innocence and honour ten thousandfold stronger than brass or Iron." Although he was embarrassed to admit it, he had even been compared, he told Mercy Warren, to Jesus Christ.[62]

One of the problems with such an exalted self-image (which recalls the old Puritan concept of sanctification) was that Adams had difficulty accepting the passions and emotions that frequently welled up within him. Take vanity. Adams would not permit it. "I am extremely unhappy to see such symptoms of . . . Vanity and Ambition as manifest themselves in Various Quarters. . . . I will neither indulge these Passions myself, nor be made the Instrument of them in others." Or suspicion. When charged with it, Adams scoffed. It was impossible—he "the most open, unsuspicious man alive, is accused of excessive suspicion." Or envy. Adams would not permit it, either. "I certainly do not abound with Envy," he told Edmund Jenings on June 8, 1779. "It is a distemper that I hope will never seize me," he repeated to James Warren on March 18, 1780.[63] But seize him it did in the wake of Franklin's elevation to sole minister. How did he handle it? By resorting to the familiar mental device of projection—the attributing of one's unacceptable feelings and ideas to others.[64]

Adams handled his envy of Franklin and his hostility toward him—the handmaiden of envy—by ascribing them to the Doctor, by concluding that Franklin was envious of and inimical to him, not he to Franklin. But he did not do this immediately after the fateful news of the dissolution of his commission arrived in Paris on February 12. During the spring and summer of 1779 he tried out various suspicions about Franklin's machinations until he came up with a theory of the Doctor's malevolence that seemed to fit the facts as he knew them.

Adams did not linger in Paris. He "was not able," he told Luzerne, "to endure the total oblivion in which I was left by the naming of Franklin minister plenipotentiary." "Nothing in the world," he continued, "could force me into contemptibility (bassesse) or to playing the role of a nullity to which I had been condemned."[65] Having settled his affairs, he withdrew his son from school and stalked off for Nantes, where he intended to embark for America. Arriving there on March 12, he discovered that the *Alliance*, on which he expected to sail, was at Brest, " 'embarrassed' with forty unruly British prisoners."[66] On March 22 he went to Brest, composed the difficulty, and returned to Nantes. On April 22 he was aboard the *Alliance*, ready to depart for America, when he received a letter from Franklin, covering one from Sartine, the French minister of the marine, informing him that the *Alliance*'s departure had been cancelled. Adams and his baggage were deposited forthwith on the dock at Nantes. Frustrated—in wandering up and down the French coast he felt "like a ghost on the banks of the Styx"—and angry, Adams had also begun to experience "some anxiety" about Congress's reaction to his departing France without leave.[67] Frustration, anger, and anxiety—than which there are fewer more potent emotional mixes—now hastened the germination of his suspicions about Franklin.

The *Alliance* had been kept at Nantes because she was to form part of an expeditionary force under the joint command of John Paul Jones and Lafayette which was to ravage the west coast of England.[68] To protect this venture, its existence was held in secrecy so tight that even an ex-commissioner like Adams was not told of it. In his distress and ignorance he began to supply reasons of his own for the *Alliance*'s cancellation. To his diary on May 12 he confided: "I am jealous that my Disappointment is owing to an Intrigue of Jones's. Jones, Chaumont, Franklin concerted the Scheme. Chaumont applied to Mr. De S[artine]. He wrote the letter . . . this Device was hit upon by Franklin and Chaumont to prevent me from going home, lest I should tell some dangerous Truths. . . . Does the old Conjurer dread my Voice in Congress? He has some Reason for he has often heard it there, a Terror to evil doers." Adams was quick to concede that he was experimenting with these suspicions: "I may be mistaken in these Conjectures, they may be injurious to J[ones] and to F[ranklin] . . . but I am determined to put down my Thoughts and see what turns out."[69] A month later after seeing the *Sensible*, the French warship on which he was to sail to America, Adams began to suspect that Franklin's putative plot had more ominous dimensions. The *Sensible* appeared to be "a dull Sailor" and since she had "but 28 Guns"—the *Alliance* had thirty-two—Adams thought she had "at least a fair Chance of rencountering an English Frigate of Superior Force, taking a share in a Sublime Battle, and being carried Captive to Hallifax or N. York, which would put it out of my Power to do good or harm for some years . . . these suppositions would give Pleasure to many, and pain to very few."[70]

With these gloomy suspicions of Franklin and his friends preying on his mind, Adams boarded the *Sensible* on June 17 and set sail for America. A mission that had started with high hopes and expectations had ended in jealousy and bitterness.

CHAPTER 3

FRANCE AGAIN, 1780

The *Sensible* crossed the Atlantic without incident and put in at Boston on August 2, 1779. A sea voyage did not improve Adams's disposition, for a friend who visited him at Braintree shortly after his arrival found him "disgusted" and "mortified" at the termination of his commission, full of "disappointment, chagrin, and vexation."[1] The people of Braintree temporarily diverted him from his problems by electing him to represent them at a convention, called for Cambridge, September 1, to prepare a constitution for Massachusetts. The convention availed itself of Adams's talents as a political theorist and made him the draftsman, the "principal Engineer," of the new constitution.[2] To one who charged that he was in a "retired and mortified" situation after returning from Europe, he responded characteristically: "I was in public forming a Constitution of Government for my country. . . . If Solon and Lycurgus were retired when they did the same for theirs, I may be said to have been retired. Instead of being mortified, it was the proudest period of my whole life. I made a Constitution for Massachusetts which finally made the Constitution of the United States."[3]

Toward the middle of October Adams learned, to his complete surprise, that on September 27 Congress had elected him minister plenipotentiary to negotiate treaties of peace and commerce with Great Britain. The appointment had been produced by an almost forgotten offer of Spain, September 29, 1778, to mediate the war between France and Britain.[4] On February 15, 1779, the French minister, Conrad Alexandre Gérard, informed Congress of the proffered Spanish mediation and urged it "to lose no time in appointing a proper person to take a part in the expected negotiation."[5] Congress, however, spent five months haggling over peace terms and by the time it formulated them, August 14, the prospect for a mediation had vanished and Spain, allied with France, was at war with Britain. Congress knew of Spain's belligerency by the end of August.[6] With the war now widened and being waged with renewed fury it made no sense to appoint a peace negotiator. But in what seemed to many an abdication of good judgment, Congress appointed Adams on September 27.[7]

In urging Adams to accept the new appointment, Elbridge Gerry called it "the highest office of Honor and Trust, under the United States." Adams, however, did not need Gerry's assistance in putting a proper value on the office. He considered it "the most important Commission" Congress had ever issued. "The Commission to General Washington as Commander-in-Chief of the army was far inferior," he believed.[8] Refusing such an honor was out of the question; of course he would return to France. But there he would be within range of Franklin again. How would the "old Conjurer" react to his returning to Europe in such an exalted state? Without even considering that in wartime, in an age of sail, it might take months for Franklin to learn of his appointment, Adams instantly assumed that Franklin would be envious of him. This conclusion, the product of Adams's projecting his own envy on the Doctor during his first mission, was reinforced by his appointment as peace commissioner, for it seemed to Adams that no man, no matter how much philosophy he was master of, could be eclipsed in the public service, as Franklin would be, without becoming envious of his successful rival. "I shall be envied more than any other," Adams wrote Arthur Lee on March 31, 1780. "To be minister at the Court of St. James is an object that will tempt numbers who would not care about any other. Nothing less than this is the Amount of my present Commission . . . the Idea of my residing in London and approaching the exalted Steps of the British Throne, I know can never be patiently born by some People." My "situation," Adams continued on April 2, "is and will be envyed."[9]

Would Franklin, consumed with envy, acquiesce in Adams's appointment? Adams feared that he would not, that he would try to "starve him out" of Europe by refusing to pay his salary and expenses. To prevent this, Adams wrote Lovell on October 25, 1779, requesting that Congress officially order Franklin to honor his requests for funds. (In the same letter Adams asked that Congress authorize him to require captains of American warships to provide him passage to the United States on demand. Never again would Franklin detain him in a dismal French seaport!) Adams repeated his demand that Congress compel Franklin to fund him in letters to Gerry of November 4 and to Lovell of November 7.[10] On February 16, 1780, he wrote his wife from Paris that if "Mr. Lovell does not procure me the Resolution of Congress I mentioned to him that of drawing on a certain Gentleman or his Banker I shall soon be starved out." A week later he predicted that there was "no Improbability at all that I may be obliged to come home again, for want of means to stay here." And on March 16 he wrote Lovell that he needed official authorization to draw funds because of those who could not "bear a Brother near the Throne, and so fair, so just, so economical a Method would not escape Minds of so much Penetration as a Refusal to lend Money without orders."[11] Adams's importunity was rewarded—and his apprehensions were accommodated—when Congress resolved, May 31: "that the establishment of the salaries of the honourable John Adams, and his secretary Mr. Dana, be transmitted to the minister plenipotentiary of these states at the Court of Versailles, and that he be directed to pay their drafts to the amount of their respective salaries."[12]

Adams seems to have borrowed the fear of being starved out from Arthur Lee and Ralph Izard. Shortly after he arrived in Paris in April 1778, Adams received a visit from Izard, who vilified Franklin, Deane, and their "French Satellites" and "represented the whole Group of them as in a Conspiracy to persecute him and the two Lees."[13] An episode that appeared to give some substance to this charge occurred a few weeks before Adams left Paris. Izard, whose commission to the Grand Duke of Tuscany was useless because the duke refused to receive him, and William Lee, commissioner to Berlin and Vienna but persona non grata at both places, whiled away their time in Paris, venting their frustrations on Franklin, who refused to consult them and scorned their gratuitous advice (Izard proposed a minatory style in dealing with the French, urging Franklin to exaggerate the plight of America and "perpetually without fatigue" to threaten the French with a rapprochement with Britain).[14] The commissioners at Paris paid the expenses of Izard and William Lee. Fed up with them at last, Franklin refused on January 13, 1779, to approve a disbursement to Lee of 34,000 livres and to Izard of 500 louis d'ors.[15] Arthur Lee put the following construction on his actions: "Jealous and irritable he easily takes offence, and pursues with secret but implacable vengeance the destruction of those who have so offended him . . . it was in this temper that he conceived an enmity against Mr. Izard, my brother and myself . . . he endeavoured to starve the two former."[16] It was to Lee, then, that Adams was evidently indebted for the suspicion that Franklin meant to starve him out.

Aside from sating his alleged malice, what would Franklin gain by removing Adams? Adams had no doubts about how the Doctor would benefit. During his first mission to France, he had discovered that, because of Franklin's transcendent reputation, "nine tenths of the public letters" were addressed to him and that he was invariably the person approached by those who wanted to discuss American affairs. Nor had the war prevented the Doctor from entertaining a stream of visitors from England,

which had given Adams "Occasion of Jealousy, however innocent the intentions were."[17] He even suspected that one of
Franklin's British callers, David Hartley, had come "with the
secret privity if not at the express request of Lord North," presumably to discuss the possibility of peace.[18] In the absence of a
duly delegated peace commission, Adams believed that Franklin
could find authorization for conducting peace negotiations in
the powers of the old three-member commission to Paris. If he
were "attacked or undermined," Adams wrote Lovell on March
16, 1780, Congress ought "to revoke the former powers of treating with all the courts of Europe which were given to the commissioners at Passy: for under these authority will be claimed of
treating with the English if my powers are revoked."[19] Franklin's
motives, then, were clear: he would starve Adams out to engross
the peace negotiations to himself. "It was," Adams later asserted, "Franklin's heart's desire to . . . strike Mr. Adams out of
existence as a public minister and get himself into his place." To
return to France, therefore, was to step into a fiery furnace. But
Adams accepted the challenge with the resolution of an early
Puritan. "I determined to go," he said, paraphrasing Martin
Luther, "though there were as many devils in the way, as there
were tiles on the houses of London."[20]

Adams embarked for France at Boston on November 13,
1779. In crossing the Atlantic, his ship sprang a leak and was
forced to put in at the Spanish port of Ferrol (December 8).
From there, he struck out for France overland. After a "journey
of near five hundred leagues, in the dead of winter, through bad
roads and worse accomodatons,"[21] he arrived at Paris on February 9. Lodgings he procured at the Hotel Valois on the Rue de
Richelieu and there he remained for the duration of his sojourn
in Paris; nothing could have persuaded him to stay with Franklin
at Passy as he had done during his first mission. During his
travels in Spain Adams had remained "on the reserve" about his
business in Europe and he maintained his silence when he arrived in Paris.[22] Franklin, in particular, must be kept ignorant of

his mission, lest he sabotage it at the start. On March 31 the Doctor wrote a friend that Adams "had never communicated anything of his business to me . . . so that I am in utter ignorance" and as late as June 13 he still was not fully informed about what Adams was up to.[23] Had Adams reflected that Franklin, ignorant of his mission, could not have been driven by envy to abort it, he could have spared himself many anxious hours, but this line of reasoning escaped him.

Keeping Franklin in the dark about his business produced some awkward moments. On February 11, for example, Adams and Franklin called on Vergennes, who must have found Adams's reticence in the presence of the Doctor mystifying. A diplomat making his first appearance at Versailles after a year's absence was expected, after all, to say something about why he was there. Adams confined himself, however, to asking the count's permission to write him about his mission. Vergennes, of course, consented. The next day Adams wrote the count, "I have *now* the honor to acquaint you, that on the 29th day of September last the Congress . . . did me the honor to elect me their plenipotentiary to negotiate a peace with Great Britain, and also to negotiate a treaty of commerce with that kingdom."[24] Vergennes now knew, but Franklin did not.

Having divulged his business in France, Adams went on in his letter to commit a fatal error. In an effort to anticipate Franklin's expected machinations, he asked Vergennes if he could communicate his powers to the British ministry. "I am the only person," he cautioned the count, "who has authority to treat of peace." "If any propositions on the part of Great Britain should be made to his Majesty's ministers," he insisted "that they be communicated to me." Adams realized how bad his eagerness to inform the British that an American peace commissioner had arrived in Europe would look. It would create the impression that the United States, despairing of success, was seeking a separate peace, in violation of the terms of its alliance with France, thus giving "just cause of jealousy to our ally."[25] He was, in fact, one of those who doubted Congress's wisdom in voting a peace mission in the fall of 1779. Though "extremely honourable" to me, the commission, he wrote on February 7, 1781, was "totally useless to the publick. It has done no good whatsoever. It has been considered as a proof of Weakness and distress and an earnest affection for Great Britain, and an ardent Wish to be restored to Friendship with them."[26]

Had Adams been privy to Vergennes's correspondence, he would have realized the magnitude of the disaster he was flirting with in proposing to communicate with the British ministry. During the spring and summer of 1779 Conrad Alexandre Gérard, the first French minister to the United States, filled his dispatches to Vergennes with the fantastic information that Samuel Adams and Richard Henry Lee were at the head of a pro-British party in Congress which sought to betray France by composing the quarrel with Britain and concluding an alliance with her. Among the members of the putative pro-British party, Gérard numbered John Adams.[27] Vergennes accepted these tales at face value, writing Luzerne on July 18, 1779, for example, of a party in Congress which "if it is not sold to England, at least favors the views of that power," a party that was trying to effect "a rapprochement between the United States and England in order to establish a separate negotiation with the court of London and to effect an alliance with that court." It was "indubitable," the count added, "that one can reckon among them Mr. John Adams."[28] Against this background, Adams's desire to communicate with the British threatened to confirm erroneous suspicion of Vergennes that he was a partisan of Britain and, potentially, a traitor to the Franco-American alliance. But there was more. On November 6 Vergennes had received from Gérard a "perfectly accurate"' summary of Adams's instructions from which he learned that the American had been charged to act "in concert" with France "in the spirit of the treaties."[29] By announcing a desire to contact the British, Adams appeared to be flouting his instructions directly in Vergennes's face and informing him in advance of his intended treachery.

How did Vergennes react to Adams's action? It has been the

contention of many historians that he was so disgusted by the letter of February 12 that he dashed off an insulting reply and set to work immediately to have Adams's "commission to negotiate a commercial treaty with Britain canceled and Adams himself neutralized by the addition of other ministers."[30] The count is supposed to have insulted Adams by forbidding him to communicate with the British and by declining to advise him further, until "the arrival of M. Gérard, because he is probably the bearer of your instructions, and will certainly be able to make me better acquainted with the nature and extent of your commission,"[31] the implication being, apparently, that Adams was too stupid to understand his own instructions. But this is false. Vergennes honestly believed that Adams did not have his instructions. He could have put two interpretations on the letter of February 12: one, consistent with Gérard's summary of Adams's instructions, was that it represented an unbelievably brazen display of bad faith; the other, that Adams appeared to be proposing separate peace negotiations out of ignorance, not malice. Vergennes chose the kinder interpretation. When Adams attempted to tell him on February 19 that he did, in fact, have his instructions, the count, though now "a little . . . puzzled," as Adams's secretary admitted,[32] assumed that Adams was being disingenuous in an attempt to cover his embarrassment at not having the instructions. Adams, the count wrote Luzerne on March 5, "has given me occasion to judge that he does not know the whole nature and whole object of his commission. . . . I hope that M. Gérard is the bearer of his instructions and I hope that they will convince him that his commission is merely eventual and that it has for its essential foundation our treaty of alliance."[33]

Had Adams been able to restrain his eagerness to communicate with the British, his mission would have had a much different issue. Vergennes was willing to give him the benefit of the doubt. The able Luzerne, having settled in Philadelphia, was soon supplying the count with more accurate information about

Adams's role in the Revolution, correcting Gérard's gross distortions. Far from being a partisan of Britain, Adams had, Luzerne reported, by his early and decided role in the Revolution rendered himself "particularly odious to the English . . . and they will find it repugnant to treat with him."[34] Had Adams simply bided his time in France, he might have won Vergennes's confidence and worked smoothly with him. But the fear of Franklin was upon him and he must inform the British of his peace commission to prevent a power grab by the Doctor. He wished, he wrote Congress on March 30, to communicate "to Lord George Germain my full powers to treat both of peace and commerce." But he would be even bolder; he would go to London in person, as Vergennes reported to Luzerne on June 3, 1780. This last proposal Adams evidently made about the time Gérard arrived in Paris from America on March 12.[35] To Vergennes, Gérard revealed that he did not have Adams's instructions. It immediately dawned on the count that he had badly misjudged Adams. The American, it now appeared, had been in possession of his instructions from the moment of his arrival and had deliberately ignored them in his haste to violate the treaty of alliance by concluding a separate peace with Great Britain.[36] Here, truly, was a wicked and dangerous man, a man whose enmity to France and partiality toward Britain were so strong that the most solemn commands of his sovereign meant nothing to him. Such a man must be controlled or, better still, removed from office.

But how could this be done? Vergennes could not ask Congress to recall Adams for violating his instructions because such a request was likely to infuriate the Americans. The instructions of a sovereign to its servants were supposed to be confidential and, by charging Adams with transgressing them, Vergennes would, in effect, be admitting that France had not scrupled to gain access to American secrets. What was needed was concrete evidence, preferably provided by Adams himself, of his insubordination. In the middle of June Adams supplied Vergennes with precisely what he wanted.

John Adams

On March 18 Congress passed a resolution pegging the value of its depreciating paper money at forty dollars paper to one dollar silver. The vigilant Luzerne informed Vergennes, April 1, that the action boded ill for France's merchants trading to the United States. Many, he declared, had already been ruined by the depreciation of American currency, for they had been compelled by a consistent inability to find return cargoes to leave the money from the sale of their merchandise in the hands of American agents, who stood by helplessly while its value evaporated in their pockets. Peace or an improvement in American military fortunes might save the French by restoring the value of their money, but Luzerne believed that the resolution of March 18 demolished these hopes and, as far as he could see, sealed the ruin of his countrymen.[37]

Luzerne's dispatch reached Paris on May 19. Whether it conveyed the first intelligence of the resolution of March 18 or whether the news of it simultaneously arrived through other channels, France's American traders were scandalized by what Congress had done and set up what Franklin on May 31 called a "great Clamour."[38] Representing their plight in terms that confirmed Luzerne's account of it, they put immediate pressure on Vergennes for relief. The count responded with an indignant letter to Luzerne of June 3, denouncing Congress for plundering the French merchants and ordering the ambassador to see that they were indemnified for their losses.[39]

Among the aggrieved French merchants was Le Ray Chaumont. On June 15, with another entrepreneur, Monthieu, in tow, he called upon Adams and complained about the injustice that he and his associates had suffered at the hands of Congress.[40] Chaumont told Adams that the French court sympathized with the merchants and suggested that he might calm the waters by using his influence with Congress to have the French excepted from the resolution of devaluation. A business associate of Deane and the friend and landlord of Franklin at Passy, Chaumont had been suspected by Adams in the spring of 1779 of intriguing with the Doctor to arrange his capture at sea. Monthieu had also done business with Deane, especially in negotiating in 1776 the famous contract to supply the Continental Army with firearms; the muskets that he sent to America were so ravaged with rust that even those in working order were more dangerous to their operators than to the enemy. Chaumont and Monthieu's association with Deane had, in fact, enrolled them in the conclave of malicious merchants which Adams believed was persecuting him and on September 10, 1779, he wrote James Lovell that he suspected that the two men were the authors of an anonymous letter, attacking him for attaching himself to "L[ee] the Madman."[41] He believed, therefore, that the two men who appeared in his office were supplicants with stilettos. They could be up to no good, of course; obviously they were concocting tales about the distress of innocent Frenchmen to enrich themselves.[42] He, apparently, was to be made a dupe to persuade Congress to line the pockets of a "Gang of Peddlars." Incensed that the Frenchmen would attempt to make him the instrument of their villainy, Adams fell on them with fury.

The resolution of March 18, he told them, was "wise, very wise, just, very just" and anyone who protested against it must be a British emissary or spy. Why, moreover, should the United States give France a special exemption from the resolution? She had "less to complain about" than any other country; she should be grateful to the United States whatever its actions "because without America to whom France does not know how to have too much obligation, England would be too powerful for the House of Bourbon."[43] Under no condition, Adams asserted, would the United States compensate or indemnify Frenchmen alleged to have been injured by the resolution of March 18, 1780.

Stung to the quick by this interview, Chaumont stalked off to Versailles and related Adams's diatribe to Vergennes. The count perceived that his opportunity to rid himself of the American was at hand. By refusing to accommodate the merchants of France, Adams had, in the count's view, put himself in direct opposition to "the sentiments of Congress relative to the French and to the alliance."[44] Vergennes liked to flatter himself that Congress was brimming with gratitude for French assistance and was disposed to do whatever favors it could for its ally, granting it, if need be, privileges that other nations and even its own citizens did not enjoy. In the matter of devaluation, for instance, the count expected Congress to press a 2.5 cent dollar on its own citizens and on the citizens of other nations but to give a Frenchman one hundred cents for his dollar. By refusing to countenance special privileges, Adams convinced Vergennes that his sentiments were contrary to those of Congress. If, he believed, he could obtain concrete evidence of Adams's perverse views, he could use it to convince Congress that Adams was misrepresenting its sentiments. Then, he hoped, the American legislature would recall its irresponsible servant.

Vergennes's problem was a nice one. How could he obtain evidence of Adams's sentiments? How could he "assure" himself "of the thinking of M. Adams?" He ordered Chaumont to write up an account of his interview with Adams but since this was only a secondhand report, it was not suitable for his purposes. Nor would an interview help. The count already knew Adams's sentiments; what he wanted was to get them on paper in his own hand. Fortunately for Vergennes, Adams himself volunteered his views by transmitting several letters "which spoke of the devaluation of the paper money."[45] Vergennes welcomed these letters because they gave him an opportunity to open a correspondence with the American minister about the morality of devaluation.[46]

On June 21 the count wrote Adams. He repeated his argument that the French merchants had been "plundered" by the resolution of March 18, told Adams that Luzerne had been instructed to protest against it, and appealed to him to use all his "endeavors to engage it [Congress] to retrace its steps, and do justice to the subjects of the King."[47] Vergennes did not have the slightest expectations that Adams would accede to this request. Chaumont had told him of the American's adamant opposition to his own entreaties and on June 19, only two days before the count composed the foregoing letter, Adams had waited on him at Versailles and had had "a long conversation" with him in which he had tried "to convince him of the rectitude" of the resolution of March 18.[48] Vergennes wrote Adams with the single intention of receiving a refusal, in his own hand, which he could use as proof that Adams's principles were opposed to the principles of the alliance as he conceived them and as he presumed Congress conceived them.

Adams fell into the count's trap because he had been eagerly seeking an opportunity to correspond with him. During his first mission he had frequently remarked upon Franklin's "indolence." Convinced that the lackadaisical Doctor was not promoting his country's interest with anything like the necessary zeal, Adams claimed, when he returned to America in the summer of 1779, that "there ought to be somebody there [in France], who knows somewhat of the affairs of America, as well as Europe, and who will take the Pains to think, and to advise the Cabinet, with all proper Delicacy, in certain Circumstances."[49] The United States had fortunately sent just such a man to France in the winter of 1780 and Adams fairly jumped at the chance to correspond with Vergennes and "to supply," as Franklin remarked later, "what he may suppose my negotiations defective in."[50]

On June 22 Adams wrote Vergennes not one, but two letters, and in both of them he praised the resolution of March 18 and steadfastly refused to assist in its emasculation. In his first letter of the day, he asked Vergennes to hold his instructions to Luzerne in abeyance "until his Excellency Mr. Franklin may have the opportunity to make his representations to his Majesty's ministers." Luzerne's instructions should be withheld "to the end that, if it should appear that those orders were issued in consequence of misinformation, they may be revoked; otherwise sent on."[51] In his second letter of the day, a production of some ten pages, Adams attempted to show Vergennes that he had, in fact, been misinformed in ordering Luzerne to protest against the devaluation resolution. The burden of his case was that no injustice had been done to the French because their American factors had manipulated the depreciating currency so cleverly that they had made huge profits for their employers. It was pointless, therefore, for Vergennes or his agent at Philadelphia to try to right a wrong that had never been.[52]

Adams was not certain that his letters would of themselves persuade Vergennes to revoke his orders to Luzerne and, therefore, in his first letter of June 22 he had asked the count to stay his orders until Franklin, whose opinion the French would respect, wrote him. But Adams was not at all sure that the Doctor would write. His letters of June 22 had dealt with matters that fell clearly within the Doctor's ministerial domain and Adams feared that if he showed them to him, Franklin would be so annoyed by Adams's encroachments that he would decline to act. Adams decided, therefore, that in order to obtain the Doctor's support for his letters of June 22, he would have to deceive him about their existence. Accordingly, on June 23 he informed Franklin that he had received a letter from Vergennes (that of June 21) "on the subject of the resolution of congress of the 18th March . . . in which his Excellency informs me that the Chevalier de la Luzerne has orders to make the strongest representations upon the subject." Would Franklin "request that those orders may be stopped, *until proper representations* can be made at Court?"[53] But what was the ten-page memorial of June 22 if not a proper representation? This little trick worked perfectly because on June 24 Franklin wrote Vergennes and requested him to withhold Luzerne's orders. Adams had contrived to obtain the Doctor's support for a memorial of whose very existence he was ignorant.

By telling Franklin in his letter of June 23 that he "firmly believed" that he could convince Vergennes of his errors in issuing Luzerne's instructions, Adams effectively prevented Franklin from writing a representation; the Doctor would obviously not write until he saw the result of Adams's efforts. This was exactly as Adams planned it because he wanted to prevent Franklin from lifting his pen. On June 29 he clinched his scheme to force inactivity upon the Doctor by showing him copies of his letters of June 22. These were, of course, so thorough that anything Franklin could have added would have been superfluous.

The reason Adams wanted to prevent Franklin from writing a representation to the French court can be gleaned from his letters to Congress of June 26 and June 29. On June 26 he treated that body to a summary of his activities during the devaluation controversy. He began by recounting his conversation of June 15 with Chaumont, who had, he claimed, been sent to him by Vergennes to consult him about the resolution of March 18; this, of course, conveyed the impression that the count considered him, and not Franklin, the man to see about American affairs.[54] Then Adams described the long conversation he had had with Vergennes on June 19. Finally, he enclosed a copy of the count's letter of June 21 and his replies of June 22. He made no mention of Franklin in the June 26 letter because he had written it to show that in the devaluation controversy he had done everything and Franklin had done nothing.

The letter of June 29 was a kind of commentary upon that of June 26. Adams informed Congress that the business of the American minister to France was "to negotiate with the Court, to propose and consult upon plans for the conduct of the war [and] to collect and transmit intelligence." There was "much reason to believe," he continued, "that if our affairs here had been urged with as much skill and industry as they might" have been, the United States "should at this moment have been blessed with peace."[55] Franklin, obviously, was not doing his job. Congress should recall him and replace him with someone more diligent, someone like John Adams, who was already on location, aggressively protecting American interests.

There was considerable irony in the devaluation controversy.

John Adams

Vergennes had provoked it to destroy Adams and Adams had tried to use it to destroy Franklin, the count's favorite American. What sharpens the irony is that Vergennes tried to make Franklin act as Adams's executioner. On June 30 the count gave the Doctor copies of all the letters that Adams and he had exchanged during the past two weeks, including his most recent one of June 30 in which he had affected anger and acridly informed Adams that "all further discussion between us on this subject [devaluation] will be needless."[56] Vergennes requested Franklin to transmit this correspondence to Congress so that that body could see how much Adams's distorted ideas about the alliance had offended the powers that be in France. This, the count hoped, would be sufficient to secure the American's recall, but in case it was not, he asked Franklin to write Congress and to support the French position. Had Franklin acceded to this request he would have had to refute his younger colleague and this was exactly what Vergennes wanted him to do, hoping no doubt that the weight of the Doctor's opinion would insure Adams's recall. Franklin refused to play the count's game and notified him on July 10 that he would do no more than transmit his correspondence with Adams to Congress.[57] Thus, the count's subtle scheme to dispose of Adams was, in a manner, thwarted. But in the month of July Adams made himself so obnoxious at Versailles that Vergennes threw subtlety to the winds and in August ordered his representative at Philadelphia to press Congress to have him recalled.

On July 2 Adams went to Versailles and broached the subject of a trip to the Netherlands. He had wanted to visit the Low Countries during his first mission and had learned, upon returning to America, that Congress had considered sending him there. Upon the eve of his departure from Boston in November 1779, he was informed, moreover, that Congress was still thinking of sending him to Holland, that he had been nominated, along with Henry Laurens, to go there to negotiate a loan.[58] Since March he had been seeking Vergennes's permission to travel to Holland—French passports were necessary to leave the king's dominions—but the count had put him off with one excuse after another, so that by July Adams had, by his reckoning, been detained in Paris for four months "wholly against my will, by the Count de Vergennes himself."[59] This time, however, Vergennes told him that he could go to Holland but asked him to wait a while because he expected in a few days to have something of importance to tell him. The count was as good as his word, summoning Adams to Versailles on July 16 to inform him that the British had sent an envoy to Madrid with whom the Spaniards had refused to confer until he obtained instructions from his government about its sentiments toward the United States; since it would take at least two months for the emissary to get information from London, Vergennes assured Adams that he would have plenty of time to take a trip to the Low Countries. The count thought that he had done the American a big favor by telling him about Sir Richard Cumberland's mission to Spain. But all he got for his "candor and loyalty" were two testy letters, one on July 13 and another on July 17.[60]

Adams's letter of July 13, described by M. Doniol as "a kind of second mémoire,"[61] was a brief on behalf of his diplomatic hobbyhorse, the establishment of French naval superiority along the coastline of North America.[62] Should France concentrate her naval power in American waters, the war, Adams explained to Vergennes, could be brought to a quick and triumphant conclusion. If the count refused to adopt this strategy, Adams threatened him with a "melancholy" reaction in America. There were, he explained, many people in the United States who wished to return "to the domination" of Great Britain and their numbers were being constantly augmented by British claims that France did not "mean to give any effectual aid to America, but only to play off her strength against that of Britain, and thus exhaust both." If France suffered these opinions to gain ground by declining to act, Adams warned that his countrymen might give up and make peace with Great Britain.[63]

Vergennes found Adams's advice gratuitous and annoying, for the strategy Adams advocated was exactly the one the count had been promoting from the beginning of the war, handicapped though he was by a smaller fleet than Britain's and opposed though he was by his ally Spain, which wanted to concentrate the naval war in Europe.[64] Convinced that Adams coveted a separate peace, Vergennes suspected that he was trying to make France's performance of an impossible task (she was incapable of maintaining naval superiority over Britain in American waters for an extended period) a test of good faith so that he might have an excuse for treating with the British. It was most unfortunate, then, that Adams should have chosen, on July 17, to press Vergennes for permission to communicate his commercial powers to the British ministry, for this simply reinforced the count's erroneous convictions. Vergennes's dander was now up and on July 25 he wrote the American minister a blistering rebuke. He began by requiring him "in the name of the King . . . to suspend . . . all steps relating to the English ministry" until Congress should have a chance to consider his proposals. Then he lit into Adams: his ideas showed "much weakness" and "much simpleness"; they were "chimerical" and would make the United States "the laughing-stock of all nations"; and they were—and this really stung—unworthy of "any thinking being."[65]

Adams should have ground his teeth and borne this abuse in silence, but he did not. He decided to repay the count in kind and on July 26 wrote him a long ill-tempered letter, rebutting him point by point, and telling him that his own reasoning fell considerably short of that of a "thinking being."[66] The next day, as if to pour salt on the wounds, Adams exhumed a letter Vergennes had written him on July 20—a letter in which the count had condescended to tell him that Louis XVI had decided to send certain naval units to America—and dissected it mercilessly.[67] This was, as Edward S. Corwin has remarked, "the straw that broke the camel's back."[68] The count, obsessed by the hobgoblin of a separate peace, believed that Adams had resorted to polemics to blow up a quarrel, to create "a Difference . . . with a view of reconciling" the United States and Great Britain and on July 29 he washed his hands of the American by brusquely informing him that he would correspond with him no longer.[69] "Mr. Franklin," he wrote, "being the sole person who has letters of credence to the King from the United States, it is with him only that I ought and can treat of matters which concern them."[70] As he had done after the devaluation controversy, Vergennes sent Adams's letters to Franklin and asked the Doctor to transmit them to Congress. But now he went much further than he had in June and on August 7 sent Luzerne a résumé of Adams's offenses to enable "the ambassador to have him recalled."[71]

The dispute with Vergennes caused the crystallization in Adams's mind of suspicions about French policy which had been taking shape for months, suspicions that reflected not only the Revolutionary mentality's fear of malign conspiracies but also the New Englander's hereditary fear of French designs to dominate his country. "Keep us poor. Depress us. Keep us weak."[72] Above all, keep America dependent on France. This was the objective Adams believed Vergennes was pursuing. The seeds of this suspicion were evidently sown by reports from London in the spring of 1780, spread to split the Franco-American alliance, that France's policy was to encourage the continuation of the war "in hopes of . . . depressing the rising power of America."[73] The charge was preposterous—in 1780 France was on the verge of bankruptcy and could so little afford another campaign that peace overtures to Lord North were made by First Minister Maurepas and, somewhat later, by Director General of Finances Necker.[74] Adams's first inclination, upon confronting the rumor, was to dismiss it out of hand, but he soon reversed himself and decided that it deserved "to be considered with all the attention that Americans can give it."[75]

There was, to begin with, Vergennes's apparent indifference

to his pleas for the establishment of French naval superiority in American waters. Why was this "short, easy, infallible method of humbling the English" rejected, if not to spin out the war and weaken America?[76] Then there were the count's rebuffs of his efforts to communicate his commercial powers to the British. In addition to his apprehensions about Franklin, Adams was governed by political considerations in wanting to communicate the commercial powers. A few weeks into his second mission, he became aware that "a good part of Europe, as well as the people of England" had been persuaded by the North ministry that "there is some secret treaty between France and the United States, by which the former have secured to themselves exclusive privileges in . . . American Commerce."[77] This was a lie, for the Continental Congress, guided by the Model Treaty of 1776, had insisted that the United States discriminate in favor of no trading nation, that it grant free and equal trade to all who reciprocated. Adams believed that if he could get this information out to the British public, he could convert it to the cause of peace, for once Britain realized that by making a treaty with the United States she would have a chance to recover much of her prewar commerce, profits, and power (as Adams was certain she would), she would have no more incentive to continue the war. In thwarting the communication of Adams's commercial powers, Vergennes surely was attempting to continue the war to America's disadvantage. And what about French loans to America? Her "monied assistance," in Adams's view, had been '"pitiful," barely enough to keep America's chin above water.[78] Finally, there were Vergennes's efforts to keep him from going to Holland (because Cumberland's mission to Spain might produce peace feelers at Paris). Impeding a trip to the Netherlands, where alternative means of support for the United States might be found, indicated only too clearly the count's desire to keep America in leading strings to France.

The manner in which Vergennes conducted diplomacy with the United States was also a signal to Adams that he meant to keep America in a condition of dependency. Vergennes's constant endeavor was to convince the Americans that benevolence and altruism motivated France's assistance to them. Let them understand, he wrote Gérard on April 22, 1778, "that we are making war only for them, that it is only because of them that we are in it."[79] In return, the count expected that Americans would treat France and her servants with effusive gratitude. Franklin was quick to see what Vergennes wanted and artfully played the role expected of him, making the expression of gratitude the touchstone of his diplomacy. It was "not only our Duty, but our Interest" to massage French egos, the Doctor wrote Congress.[80]

Adams found it impossible to imitate Franklin. He was deeply suspicious of Vergennes's efforts to "Make us feel our Obligations [to] Impress our Minds with a Sense of Gratitude." Never in his life, he wrote his wife on December 18, 1780, had he "observed any one endeavouring to lay me under particular obligations to him, but I suspected he had a design to make me his dependant, and to have claims upon my gratitude."[81] So, beneath Vergennes's diplomatic style, there appeared to lurk a sinister design to reduce Adams—and America—to a demeaning dependency.

In dealing with Vergennes, Adams adopted a diplomatic style to accommodate these apprehensions. His objective was to banish gratitude from the diplomatic dialogue between France and the United States because of the danger "that too much will be demanded of us" if Americans assumed the role of obsequious beneficiaries which Vergennes had picked for them. Interest, which Adams believed "alone" governed the councils of men, must supplant gratitude as the guiding principle of Franco-American diplomacy.[82] To Adams, it was indisputable that France was supporting the United States purely from motives of self-interest: it was "because England is the natural Enemy of France, that America in her present Situation is her natural Friend," he wrote in 1779. Therefore, he believed that self-interest should be stressed in dealing with Vergennes: "State the interest France had in supporting us . . . and not make it a matter of mere grace." In applying for French naval support, for example, he emphasized to the count that upon "principles of French interest and policy alone" a fleet should be "constantly kept in North America."[83] If putting Franco-American relations on the foundation of self-interest was an effective way to forestall French claims on American gratitude, it was also a rebuke to Vergennes, whose emphasis on French benevolence was made to appear hypocritical. The count, naturally enough, resented Adams's diplomatic style.

Adams's ideas about the obligations between the two partners in the alliance also annoyed Vergennes. His belief in America's decisive role in the European balance of power gave offense here, for the French foreign minister did not relish being told that the power of a united British Empire would have been "fatal" to his country. By breaking with Britain and allying themselves with France, the Americans had delivered France from the heel of an "imperious master," had raised her from the "Contempt, Misery, and Debasement in which Louis 15 left it, to a Pitch of Reputation, opulence, and Power." It followed, then, that France did "not know how to have too much obligation" to the United States, that she was "more oblig'd to us than we to her." According to Silas Deane (who returned to France in the summer of 1780), Adams asserted "not only in private but in his letters to the Minister" that "America is not obliged to France, but the contrary." As a result, he believed that the United States need not approach France with the trembling gratitude of a client but was justified in treating her as an equal. Therefore, when Vergennes abused him in July, he replied in kind, answering the count "huff for huff."[84]

But huffing, Adams perceived, was not the best way to defeat Vergennes's putative designs. Other sources of support must be enlisted and, with this in mind, he left Paris on July 27, 1780, for the Netherlands "to try," as he told Franklin, "whether something might not be done to render us less dependent on France."[85] Franklin, who had been on the sidelines while the Adams–Vergennes battle raged, was nevertheless one of its casualties. The Doctor had always preached against Congress's flooding Europe with unwelcome diplomats. He had "constantly declared," within Adams's hearing, "that congress was wrong in sending a minister to Berlin, Vienna, Tuscany, Spain, Holland and Petersburg." "A Virgin State," he believed, should "preserve its Virgin Character and not go about Suitoring for Alliances."[86] At first, these sentiments seemed innocent enough to Adams; in fact, he agreed with them, advising Lovell from Paris on January 3, 1779, "to recall, every Commissioner, you have in the World, excepting one to this Court and to Spain."[87] But in the summer of 1780, in the context of what Adams took to be Franklin's envious machinations against him, the Doctor's recommendations looked very different. What psychologists call the process of retroactive falsification seems to have come into operation, by which "incidents of the past receive a new interpretation and are fitted into the framework of present persecution."[88] Because Franklin had formerly opposed scattering ministers around Europe, Adams now assumed that he was against his going to Holland. Why would the Doctor want to obstruct him? Envy, of course. He wanted, it appeared, to "sweep Europe clean of every Minister but himself, that he might have a clear unrivalled Stage," sweep Europe clean lest "someone would serve his Country, acquire a Reputation, and begin to be thought of by Congress to replace him."[89]

Both Vergennes and Franklin evidently wanted to keep Adams out of Holland. Was this a mere coincidence? Adams was sure it was not. The cloying gratitude with which the Doctor treated the count—excessive "diffidence" and "servile Complaisance" in Adams's view—and the exaggerated deference that Vergennes and his understrappers showed Franklin convinced Adams that the two men were confederates in a conspiracy against him, that they had, in fact, formed an "Alliance"

John Adams

against him, each wishing, for his own reasons, to defeat his Dutch mission.[90] Thus, as we follow Adams to Amsterdam, we should be aware of the way in which he viewed his errand: he "was pursued into Holland by the intrigues of Vergennes and Franklin, and was embarrassed and thwarted, both in my negotiations for a loan and in those of a political nature, by their friends, agents, and spies, as much, at least, as I ever had been in France."[91]

CHAPTER 4

THE NETHERLANDS

Adams left Paris on July 27, passed through Brussels, Antwerp, Rotterdam, and The Hague and arrived in Amsterdam on August 10, 1780, where he lived for the next twenty months. The decision to settle in Amsterdam was ill advised. True, as the financial capital of Holland, it was the place to negotiate a loan, which would lessen American dependence on France. But Adams's objective in the Netherlands extended beyond borrowing money. Always considering his peace commission his primary trust, he wanted to do something in Holland to "accelerate" peace negotiations. Therefore, his objective in the Netherlands was, in its broadest sense, political, and political business was best conducted, not in Amsterdam, but in the nation's capital, The Hague, "the eye and heart of continental politics," as one of Adams's associates called it.[1]

But there was, in Adams's view, an insuperable objection to settling at The Hague: it was the residence of the French ambassador, the Duke de la Vauguyon, the incarnation in Holland, he believed, of Vergennes's scheme to reduce America to a demeaning dependency on France. Adams treated Vauguyon precisely as he had Franklin in February 1780: he told him nothing and stayed as far away from him as possible. Passing through The Hague on the morning of August 9, Adams had a "short and general" conversation with Vauguyon,[2] hurried on to Amsterdam, and did not see the French ambassador again until the following April. American affairs in The Hague Adams left in the hands of C. W. F. Dumas, an impecunious Swiss intellectual—he later took employment as a majordomo in Adams's house—whom Franklin had recruited some years earlier as an American agent.[3] Dumas knew little about the conventions of conducting foreign policy in the Netherlands—not until March 21, 1781, for example, did he discover that memorials of foreign ministers were submitted to the grand pensionary of Holland (the Dutch equivalent of a secretary of state) as well as to the president of the States General—but his amateurishness concerned Adams far less than James Lovell's warning that he was "all-together an Instrument in the hands of Deane and Franklin."[4] Thus, rather than being part of the solution Adams sought in Holland, Dumas was part of the problem and Adams was content to leave him at The Hague.[5]

By isolating himself from Vauguyon, Adams forfeited the opportunity of informing himself of the objectives of French diplomacy in the Netherlands. Knowledge of French aims might well have lessened his suspicions of their malevolence. In forgoing a liaison with the French ambassador, Adams also cut himself off from the most likely source of information about Dutch politics, for Dutch politicians, especially after relations with Britain took a decisive turn for the worst in December 1780, avoided Adams "like a pestilence," as he put it.[6] As late as January 25, 1781— six months into his mission—he apparently had not been able to meet a single member of the States General.[7] The conduct of the pensionary of Amsterdam, van Berckel, was typical: "He dared not," Adams said, "have any communications with me. I made a visit to his house, but was denied admittance. I wrote him letters, but received no answer. He was reduced to the necessity of writing secretly to Mr. Dumas, to pray to make his apology to me, and to say that, though he was very desirous to see me, and to answer my letters, he dared to do neither—'because everything possible was being done to sacrifice me to the Anglomanes.' "[8] The few Dutch politicians who would see Adams were outcasts like Baron van der Capellen, a "nervous and vulnerable" man, who spoke darkly of "enemies," of "tyrants," who had expelled him from the states of Overijssel.[9]

Isolated from French and Dutch sources of reliable political information, Adams also found no American who could serve as a political confidant, no one on whom he could rely to validate his conclusions and correct him when he was wrong. The secretary to the peace commission, Francis Dana, could have filled this function, but Adams left him behind in Paris to transact whatever business arose there. It is a commonplace observation that "isolation and limited communication deprives" a person "of reality checks that modify his distorted views."[10] Being in precisely this situation in the Netherlands, Adams's suspicions flourished and became almost paranoid in their intensity. His conviction, moreover, that he was the object of an unremitting French and "Franklinian" conspiracy frequently caused him to exaggerate his own importance and to magnify his activities into dimensions that were, at times, grotesque.

Settling in Amsterdam removed Adams from Vauguyon's orbit, but did not, initially, put him at ease. His suspicions heightened by unfamiliar surroundings, he quickly concluded that the hotel where he stayed for the first two days in Amsterdam (August 10-12) was overrun with enemy agents.[11] In fact, Adams spent few days in Europe without voicing the fear that he was being observed by spies. "There are Spies upon every Word I utter, and every Syllable I write," he informed his wife on February 20, 1779—"Spies planted by the English—spies planted by Stock-jobbers—spies planted by selfish Merchants—and spies planted by envious and malicious Politicians."[12] (Spies, indeed, were swarming in the capitals of European diplomacy and finance. Adams's fears of them, however, were not based on deductions from the conduct of individuals, but were curiously generalized and indiscriminate. He never suspected, moreover, the duplicity of Edward Bancroft, the most remarkable double agent of the

John Adams

era, and there is reason to believe that his own trusted confidant, Edmund Jenings, was, unbeknownst to him, a British agent.[13]) To escape the "observation of spies," Adams withdrew from the Arms of Amsterdam after two days and took rooms in a private house. But even here he was not entirely safe, for it was soon noised about that his lodgings were too obscure for an American diplomat. These complaints, he believed, were "put into circulation by English spies."[14]

In Amsterdam, Adams set about to verify reports which had reached him in Paris that the United States could borrow money in the Netherlands. To his initial inquiries he received such optimistic replies that he wrote Congress on August 14 that he was sure he could obtain a loan from the Dutch. On September 16 he received from Congress a commission to borrow money, to be effective until minister-designate for the Netherlands, Henry Laurens, arrived. He immediately sought out those people who had encouraged him earlier, but they changed their tune and now informed Adams that a loan would be difficult to negotiate until the States General recognized American independence.[15] A loan, in other words, was as much a political question as a financial one. Indeed, it was altogether a political question, for, as Vauguyon discovered, even if the interest and principal of a loan to the United States were guaranteed jointly by the king of France and the states of Holland (thus making it absolutely safe), the Dutch would not touch it until it was "determined what characters are to bear rule and what system is to prevail."[16]

The political system in the Netherlands in the fall of 1780 was in a state of fermentation. The war for American independence created friction between the Dutch and the British, allies for over a century. Britain objected to the Americans' supplying themselves at the Dutch West Indian island of Saint Eustatia and, after France entered the war in 1778, to Dutch insistence on furnishing her with naval stores, as the Anglo-Dutch treaty of 1674 gave her the right to do. In the spring of 1780 the British denounced the treaty of 1674 and began seizing Dutch ships car-

rying contraband (as the British defined it) to France. The Dutch
sought refuge from the British depredations in the Armed Neutrality, the association for the protection of maritime rights, announced by Catherine II of Russia on February 28, 1780.[17] Invited by Catherine to join the Armed Neutrality on April 3, the
Dutch tried for months to exact from Russia a guarantee of their
colonial possessions as a precondition for accepting the invitation. Failing to receive the guarantee (September 11), the Dutch
paused, pondered, and moved in the direction of joining the
new league. The British, unaware, as yet, that the Armed Neutrality would be an "Armed Nullity," as Catherine herself called
it, sought desperately for a pretext to prevent the Dutch from
putting their shipping under its protection. On September 3 the
Royal Navy fished one out of the waters of the North Atlantic.

Henry Laurens sailed from Philadelphia for his post in the
Netherlands on August 13, 1780. His ship was taken by H.M.S.
Vestal on September 3. Laurens threw his papers into the sea,
but some, insufficiently weighted, were retrieved by his captors.
Among them was a "treaty," negotiated between William Lee
and the Amsterdam merchant Jean de Neufville at Aix-la-
Chapelle in the summer of 1778. Neither de Neufville, who was
acting as the representative of van Berckel, pensionary of Amsterdam, nor Lee had any authority to bind their respective
countries, so that the "treaty" was merely the wishful thinking
of two dabblers in diplomacy.[18] The British, however, chose to
construe it as evidence that the Dutch government was interfer-
ing with their rebellious colonial subjects. On November 10 the
king's ambassador at The Hague, Sir Joseph Yorke, delivered an
indignant ultimatum to the States General, demanding that it
disavow van Berckel and punish him in an exemplary way; otherwise, Yorke threatened, George III would "take such measures
as he shall think the dignity and essential interests of his people
require."[19] Yorke's ultimatum destroyed whatever hopes Adams
still had of borrowing money, for as he told James Warren on
December 9, no Dutchman would deal with him "lest England

John Adams

should declare war against them for aiding, abetting and comforting Rebellion."[20]

The States General promptly disavowed van Berckel's conduct but refused to punish him. On November 20 it voted to accede unconditionally to the Armed Neutrality. On December 14 Yorke presented a second memorial, insisting on the punishment of van Berckel. The States General went into special session and on December 22 referred the pensionary's problem to the Supreme Court of Holland. In the meantime, the British ministry got word of the Dutch accession to the Armed Neutrality (December 18) and on December 20 it issued, at Saint James, a manifesto, reciting its grievances against the Dutch, announcing the withdrawal of Yorke from The Hague, and stating its intention "to pursue such vigorous measures as the occasion fully justifies." Simultaneously, an order-in-council was issued "authorizing reprisals against Dutch shipping and property." Although the manifesto of December 20 was not, technically, a declaration of war, the distinction was lost on Dutch shippers who were treated by the British as open enemies.[21]

The manifesto of December 20 produced what Adams described as a "violent shock" in the Netherlands, causing even the best men to "shudder with fear." "Every party, and every man almost," he wrote Francis Dana on January 18, 1781, "is afraid to do the least thing that England can complain of and make a noise about, lest the blame of involving the country in a war should be thrown upon them." In these circumstances a loan was out of the question, a fact that Adams stressed to Congress: "I have no hopes at present of obtaining money" (January 4); "There is as yet no possibility of borrowing any money" (January 14).[22] A loan would fail—that was certain; yet in February Adams opened one for the United States. The only person who would manage it was de Neufville, already a pariah because of his "treaty" with Lee. De Neufville was an imprudent merchant–financier, whose affairs in 1781 already displayed the symptoms of distress which forced him to flee to the Duchy of

The Netherlands

Cleves in 1782. A Dutch financier, one Bicker, warned Adams about him when he first arrived in Holland; so bad, in fact, was his reputation that Vergennes forbade Vauguyon to have any dealings with him.[23] A desperate man enlisting in a desperate cause, de Neufville was characteristic of the handful of Dutchmen who associated with Adams during the period when he was being shunned like a "pestilence."

On February 19 de Neufville opened a loan for one million guilders. It failed abysmally; six months later three people had pledged three thousand guilders. What impelled Adams to try an experiment he knew would be futile? Apparently it was the Argus-eyed spies whom he believed were surrounding him. "I had spies enough upon me from England, France, and America too, very ready to impute blame to me. Congress were constantly drawing upon me and there was the utmost danger that their bills would be protested. If this event should happen, I knew that representations in private letters would go to America and to France, that this fatal calamity was wholly owing to my negligence and obstinacy in refusing to open a loan in M. de Neufville's house." Fear of persecution, therefore, drove Adams to open a loan that was so clearly foredoomed that Dutch observers questioned his good sense. Why would anyone approve an enterprise so "useless," so "extremely foolish"?[24]

The British commencement of hostilities against the Netherlands prompted the Dutch to appeal to Russia (January 12, 1781), which had pledged to defend any nation attacked as a result of its accession to the Armed Neutrality. Like most people in the Netherlands, Adams believed that Catherine and her allies would assist the Dutch. At any moment he expected to see "Russia, Sweden, Holland, France, Spain and America all at war against England at once." If he could persuade the Armed Neutrals, now become belligerents, to acknowledge the independence of the United States, not only would its dependence on France be lessened, but a peace negotiation might result, for would Britain not see the futility of continuing to repress a people whose independence had been so widely recognized?[25]

That Adams had no powers to treat with the Armed Neutrals did not daunt him; he believed that his powers to negotiate a loan could be stretched to conduct a negotiation as promising as one that would enlist the Armed Neutrality on America's side. Accordingly, on February 2 he informed Dumas at The Hague that, in his opinion, the time had come to employ article 10 of the Franco-American alliance, which stipulated that France and the United States could invite other nations "who may have received injuries from England to make common cause with them." On February 5 Dumas replied that such an action would "embarrass" the States General; it would be better, he continued, to suspend any overtures until the political situation became clearer. The French ambassador, Dumas added, endorsed his opinion. Just what Adams expected! France would oppose any maneuver that could lessen America's dependence on it and, playing Franklin's game, would attempt to deprive him of the opportunity, in the Netherlands as well as in France, of playing a political role. Dutch recognition of American independence—or, better still, the Armed Neutrality's recognition, "the End and Aim" of Adams's existence—would have to be gained, it appeared, over unyielding French opposition.[26]

Had Adams not estranged himself from Vauguyon, he would have known that France favored Dutch recognition of American independence as being in her own as well as in the United States' interest. Vergennes, it is true, received the news of Laurens's appointment to negotiate a treaty with the Dutch (November 1, 1779) with disdain. Were the Dutch, at peace in 1779 and 1780, to treat with Laurens, they would invite a war with Britain which they wished at all costs to avoid; in the count's eyes, therefore, Congress was foolish and irresponsible to give Laurens a commission for the Netherlands. But after Britain initiated hostilities against the Dutch, Vergennes instructed Luzerne at Philadelphia, January 9, 1781, to recommend that Congress send an emissary "with full powers" to The Hague; on

February 19 he ordered his minister to urge Congress "to prepare without loss of time the way for a coalition" with the Dutch and empowered him to say that "the King authorizes you, Monsieur, to offer to Congress his good offices to effect that end."[27]

Franco-American objectives in Holland were not to be accomplished by high-pressure public diplomacy. This Vergennes repeatedly made clear to Vauguyon. The complexities of the Dutch political system made The Hague a difficult assignment for any minister, but it was especially difficult for a minister of France, whose power had been in eclipse for so long in the Low Countries. Sent to The Hague in 1776, Vauguyon assiduously cultivated politicians in the so-called Patriot party, which opposed the pro-British stadtholder. In time, Vauguyon acquired an extraordinary ascendancy over the Patriots—Bemis called him their "whip"—on which all observers of the Dutch scene commented.[28] Vergennes congratulated his ambassador on "the popularity which you enjoy in Holland"; a British agent remarked that Vauguyon held the "key to the cabinet" of Dutch politics; a Dutch opponent complained that Vauguyon "played with" his countrymen "like children." Perhaps Frederick the Great paid Vauguyon the highest compliment; wishing to check the inroads of the Patriots against the prerogatives of his nephew, the stadtholder, Frederick instructed his ambassador, Thulemeyer, to ask Vauguyon to intercede with them and restrain them.[29]

Vauguyon was obliged to develop an impressive network of personal relationships to implement the policy of finesse and manipulation which Vergennes prescribed for him. French policy in the Netherlands, Vergennes continuously stressed, was to be one of "circumspection."[30] He meant that France was to make no public demands on the Dutch for their cooperation; rather they were to be managed so that, of their own initiative, they would propose policies that France wanted them to follow. Vauguyon was to refrain from making demands on the Dutch for two reasons: they would make unacceptable counterdemands

John Adams

and they were pro-British. Having depended for so many years on British military protection, the Dutch, by 1778, had allowed their armed forces to fall into complete decay.[31] This meant that they had no way to protect their rich colonial empire, which an opponent could capture as he pleased. Were France to invite the Dutch to become allies or to make any other move (like recognizing American independence) which would incite Britain to hostilities, the Dutch would require that France, in return, protect their colonial possessions (as they insisted that Russia do as a precondition of their participation in the Armed Neutrality). Not wishing to assume such a burden, Vergennes abstained from requesting anything from the Dutch.

Dutch bias toward Britain also influenced the count. The testimony on this point is overwhelming. The correspondence of both Adams and Vergennes is full of fears that the Dutch, as a result of ingrained affection for Britain, would make a humiliating peace with her.[32] "The utmost expectation," Adams wrote Robert Livingston on February 20, 1782, "that many of the well-intentioned have entertained, has been to prevent the government from joining England." Admiration for Britain produced suspicion of France. Wrote Benjamin Waterhouse, a member of the Adams household in 1781: the "character of the French politicians was so firmly Reviled in Holland that when . . . they [the Dutch] were at war with England, and at peace with France their jealousy and dislike were stronger towards France than toward England."[33] Attuned to the feelings of the Dutch, Vergennes feared that any heavy-handed pressure on them to take France's side against Britain would be counterproductive, would drive them into the arms of the British. Thus, he wrote Vauguyon on January 9, 1781, it was necessary to "redouble our circumspection" lest British partisans among the Dutch "envisage our insinuations as the result of a project to engage the Republic in our quarrel and to aid us with its resources for the success of our views and thus furnish a motive to alter the confidence which our moderate system could not fail to inspire."[34]

Vergennes believed that American diplomacy in the Netherlands must fit into the system of circumspection. The Dutch—and all Europe, for that matter—regarded the United States as a French client, whose every move was dictated by Versailles. The Prussian ambassador, for example, alluding in April 1781 to Adams's diplomatic activities, concluded that "the minister of France had resumed his project to tie the Republic to the American confederacy." Vauguyon knew that the United States was regarded as a French stalking-horse, that the Dutch would consider American diplomatic initiatives as being "excited in an underhanded way" by the French. Therefore, he believed it his duty, as well as in the joint interest of France and America, to discourage any public diplomacy by Adams which was inconsistent with his own; were Adams to flout his advice and go public, Vauguyon believed himself obliged to inform the Dutch that his conduct was repudiated by France.³⁵ To Adams, who had deliberately chosen to be uninformed about the motives of Vauguyon's diplomacy, French circumspection appeared to be anti-American, appeared as a refusal to support his own and his country's aspirations, and as confirmation, therefore, of his convictions that France wished to keep America dependent by obstructing a recognition of her independence by the Dutch and the Armed Neutrals.

Two days after being discouraged from employing article 10 of the Franco-American alliance, Adams received, from Dana in Paris, dispatches from Congress. Among them was a letter from James Lovell of December 12, 1780, enclosing a resolution which Congress had taken that day, thanking Adams for his "industrious attention to the interest and honor of the United States" in his correspondence with Vergennes over the devaluation of American paper money. Since Adams was "prepared in my own mind to receive from Congress resolutions of a different nature"—"resolutions of recal or at least censure," he added later, "upon the petulant and groundless complaint of Vergennes," the commendation of December 12 was a tonic to his spirits. It

John Adams

convinced him that, in dealing with the French foreign minister, he had been "possessed of the true principles of Congress" (he did not know that on its way from Congress was a rebuke, January 10, for disagreeing with Vergennes about communicating his peace powers to the British) and enabled him to assume that he had congressional carte blanche to flout French advice. Immediately, he began to conduct a more aggressive diplomacy.[36]

Among the dispatches received from Dana on February 7, 1781, was a journal of Congress, containing a resolution of October 5, directing the American navy, in its treatment of neutral shipping, to adhere to the principles of the Armed Neutrality and authorizing American ministers abroad to subscribe to these principles if invited. Hoping to attract the attention of the Armed Neutrals, Adams immediately published the resolution in Cerisier's *Amsterdam Gazette*. From The Hague, Dumas protested his precipitation, admonishing him that "the Ambassador of our Ally thinks as I do." More evidence that France meant to obstruct the American cause! Confirmation of Adams's convictions on this point kept coming to him. The refusal of Spain to recognize American independence was constantly cited by the Dutch to justify their own reserve toward the United States. "The constant cry is, 'why is Spain silent? We must wait for Spain.' "[37] Adams believed that Vergennes controlled Spanish diplomacy—as egregious a misconception as he ever entertained[38]—and that the count was restraining Spain from recognizing American independence. "I know the reason" for Spanish reluctance "very well," he informed a correspondent on February 9, "but I cannot tell it." Commenting later on this letter, Adams remarked, "I then believed, and I still believe, that the policy of the Count de Vergennes, which exerted all its resources through the duke de la Vauguyon at the Hague, to embarrass me . . . was employed at Madrid through the count Montmorin to retard Mr. Jay, for his fundamental and universal principle appeared to be to keep us entirely dependent on France."[39]

The Netherlands

On February 25 Adams received from Congress a commission to negotiate a treaty of amity and commerce with the Dutch government and an authenticated copy of the resolution of October 5. He lost no time in putting the new powers into effect. On March 8 he sent to Dumas at The Hague a memorial for presentation to the States General, announcing that he was the American minister plenipotentiary, communicating the resolution of October 5 and requesting that he be allowed to subscribe to the Armed Neutrality. To the ministers of Russia, Sweden, and Denmark–Norway he sent similar communications. Finally, he wrote Vauguyon, asking his support.[40]

Adams chose an inopportune time for his demarche. In response to the Dutch request for assistance of January 12, 1781, Russia on March 1, offered to mediate their dispute with the British. It was a foregone conclusion that the Dutch, who, Adams observed on March 12, were "furious for peace," would accept the mediation, which they did on March 14.[41] But would Great Britain also accept? The surest means to dissuade her was to arouse her ire by bringing to her attention another example of Dutch dealings with her rebellious American subjects. Yet here came Adams, as Britain balanced the question of whether to accept the mediation, with a proposal at least as embarrassing to the Dutch as the Lee–de Neufville "treaty" of 1778. Their response was to suppress the memorial. Dumas, who presented it on March 10, warned Adams "that such could well be the case, when England has still not given a response to the overtures of Russia." Dumas, in fact, could not discover what had become of the memorial until the middle of April, when he was told that it was "laid aside subject to a new order."[42]

To Adams's request that he support his memorial, Vauguyon replied on March 14 by letter (the two men still had not met since the preceding August) that he was "persuaded, Monsieur, that you will perfectly feel the impossibility of seconding it without an express order of the king."[43] Vauguyon opposed Adams's action not only because it would embarrass the Dutch but also because it threatened to jeopardize France's relations with Russia, one of the keystones of her diplomatic system. In March 1781 Russia was offering to mediate on two fronts: separately, between Britain and the Netherlands and, jointly, with Austria, between France and Spain on one side and Britain on the other. France expected Catherine II to favor her in the mediation with Britain and therefore made it a cardinal rule throughout 1781 and 1782 not "to do anything against the views of Russia."[44] Were Adams's demarche to inflame the British and sabotage the Dutch mediation, Vauguyon feared that Russia would blame France, as patron of the Americans, and might, in a pique, refuse to support the Franco-American position in the mediation with the British. Therefore, Vauguyon tried to undo the damage of Adams's demarche, undertaking, among other things, to inform Dutch officials, "I had no knowledge of it and that M. Adams had told me about it only after having done it."[45]

Vauguyon's opposition did not, of course, surprise Adams; "knowing the game of the Count de Vergennes and his ambassador, it was," he said later, "precisely what I expected."[46] But anticipation of the rebuff did not mitigate it. By March 1781, in fact, Adams began to feel that the continued opposition of, first, Vergennes and then of Vergennes and Vauguyon in tandem to his efforts to play a public role was relentless and unbearable. The forces arrayed against him seemed to grow satanic. No longer did he fear only the machinations of spies. By the spring of 1781 he felt that he was in danger of being "torn to pieces by an enraged populace," of being "hanged" by a "mob" manipulated by malefactors.[47] He even began to imagine that he was being "menaced" by Franklin for wishing to deploy his plenipotentiary powers, although the Doctor did not know that he had them.[48] The constant frustration he had experienced acted, moreover, like a bellows on his anger, blowing it up to towering heights. A member of his household at the time marveled how he "waxed wroth" and declared that he should never "forget his paroxysms of patriotic rage."[49] By the spring of 1781

Adams can best be compared to a man enduring the medieval English ordeal of *peine dure et forte*, in which heavy rocks were piled upon a victim's chest until he confessed a crime or died. The pressure of the accumulated French and Franklinian enmity (no matter that it was delusive) had become so insufferable that Adams must either overcome it with an act of heroic self-assertion or be destroyed.

Adams's assertion took the form of a second memorial to the States General, announcing once again that he was minister plenipotentiary to the Netherlands and requesting that the Dutch negotiate a treaty of amity and commerce with him. Adams worked up the new memorial with care—three drafts exist in his papers—because he proposed to give it the widest possible circulation. Having satisfied himself with it, he gave it to Dumas who on April 13 completed a French translation for presentation to the appropriate Dutch officials. Adams intended to go to The Hague to present the memorial in person and evidently contemplated ignoring Vauguyon, fearing that it would set a bad precedent to consult him. Dumas, however, urged him at least to acquaint Vauguyon verbally of what he proposed to do. Instead, Adams wrote the duke on April 16, informing him that he had received commissions and letters of credence to the Dutch but saying nothing more. Vauguyon responded the next day, professing ignorance of whether Adams intended to make a public demarche but requesting a conference with him if he did.[50] On April 19, the anniversary of Lexington and Concord, Adams signed the memorial and went to the French embassy at The Hague, where for two hours Vauguyon attempted to talk him out of presenting it. At eight o'clock the next morning, the duke appeared at Adams's hotel and for four more hours reasoned, cajoled, and pleaded with him to reconsider his plans.[51] But to no avail. In the spirit of the Massachusetts militia at Lexington, Adams was determined to conquer or die.

What did the two men say on April 19-20? For the most part, they seemed to have talked past each other. Believing that his "whole system in Holland, and even my residence in it, was disagreeable" to the French, supposing, moreover, that Vauguyon "had instructions from the Count [de Vergennes] to counteract me," Adams regarded Vauguyon's learned disquisitions on the diplomatic realities as "mere pretexts" to cover French hostility to him and did not heed them.[52]

For his part, Adams did not divulge to Vauguyon his reasons for presenting the memorial. "I saw myself ill-treated and persecuted by a set," he explained confidentially to Lovell. "I own I seized with pleasure, so fair, so great an opportunity, of giving to my own character a reputation and publicity, which should place it out of the reach of all the little shafts of malice, envy, and revenge." Nor did Adams mention the hostile mobs from whose aggressions he believed the memorial would protect him. He should, he assured Robert Livingston in February 1782, have "met with many disagreeable scenes, if not public affronts" had he not acted. His "openness" had protected him. "No one would dare offer any insult to her [America's] minister, as soon as he should be known." Refusing to reveal these, his real motives, what Adams told Vauguyon to justify his actions struck the duke as "very vague reasonings which do not appear to have any foundation."[53]

Trying as the interviews with Vauguyon were, Adams kept his temper. And no matter how hard the duke pressed him, his resolution never flagged. The conclusion of the interview was dramatic:

> At last, when he [Vauguyon] found I was not convinced, he desired me to postpone my visit to the president of their High Mightinesses, until he could write to the Count de Vergennes, and have his opinion. I answered, by no means. Why? Because I know beforehand the Count's opinion will be point blank against me; and I had rather proceed against his judgement, without officially knowing his opinion, than with it, as I am determined in all events to go. The Duke had one resource still left. It was, to persuade me to join him in

writing, or let him alone write a request to the King of
France, that he would order his ambassadors to unite
with me in my endeavors to obtain an acknowledgment
of my public character. I answered again, by no means.
"Why?" "Because, Monsieur le Duc, if I must speak out
in plain English or plain French, I know the decision of
the King's council will be directly and decidedly against
me; and I am decidedly determined to go to the president, though I had a resolution of the King in council
against me and before my eyes. . . ." "Are you willing
to be responsible, then?" "Indeed, I am; and upon my
head may all the consequences of it rest." "Are you
then determined?" "Determined, and unalterably
determined I am."[54]

Adams had not planned to present his memorial immediately
after consulting Vauguyon. He intended to wait until May 4,
1781, the date on which the assembly of the most influential
Dutch province, Holland, met, concurrently with the States
General, at The Hague. In the fortnight between April 20 and
May 4 the emotional strain of the confrontation with Vauguyon
began to tell on Adams. He evidently began to have second
thoughts about the rectitude of the action he proposed to take.
Vauguyon's arguments against it kept recurring, especially his
statement, backed by the weight of his wide connections in the
Netherlands, that those "patriots whose zeal for the American
cause ought to be known to him [Adams] . . . have strongly assured him [Vauguyon] that they were unanimously of the same
opinion as I." Adams later told Robert Livingston that he had
"the Secret advice of our best friends in the republic" to present
the memorial, but he must have realized that his advisers were
hardly more than a conventicle of the radical fringe in Dutch
politics. Consequently, the Adams who presented the memorial
on May 4, 1781, was a picture, not of intrepid energy but of
emotional turmoil. The American physician Benjamin Waterhouse, who lived in his household at the time, described how

Adams "had hardly spoken to us for days before—such was his inexpressible solicitude," that leaving the house "with protuberant eyes and holding his memorial in his hands," he "said to us, in a solemn tone—Young men! remember this day—for this day I go to the Hague to put seed in the ground that may produce Good or Evil—God knows which—and putting the paper into his side-pocket, he stepped into his coach, and drove off alone."[55]

At The Hague Adams attempted to present his memorial to the grand pensionary of Holland, van Bleiswyck, to the president of the States General, Linden de Hemmen, and to the secretary of the Prince of Orange, Baron de Ray. None of these worthies would receive it, although the president of the States promised to communicate the nature of his visit to his colleagues. Adams then turned to the printing presses. Thousands of copies of the memorial were issued in English, French, and Dutch. One was sent to "every member of the constitutional sovereignty in all the Provinces—a total of between four and five thousand persons."[56] Copies were lavished on Dutch newspapermen as well.

What was the impact of the memorial? Adams took two somewhat contradictory views. On the one hand, he argued that the fervor of Vauguyon's opposition to it proved its significance. "The earnest opposition made by the Duc de la Vauguyon," he wrote some months later, "only served to give me a more full and ample persuasion and assurance of the utility and necessity of the measure," i.e., of presenting the memorial. Thus, he argued, it was altogether possible that his memorial had produced the Dutch naval victory over the British at the Doggersbank in the North Sea in August 1781, that it had encouraged Emperor Joseph II of Austria to declare religious liberty in his dominions, and that it had insured the success of John Laurens's special mission to France in the spring of 1781. "I shall forever believe that it contributed to second and accelerate Colonel Laurens' negotiation," he wrote.[57] The fact was that the loan "obtained" by Laurens had been promised to Franklin by Vergennes well before the colonel arrived in France in March 1781,[58] two months before Adams presented his memorial. His other claims on the memorial's behalf were even more farfetched.

At other times, however, Adams took a more modest view of the memorial. During his Dutch mission and for some time thereafter he adopted the view that no American diplomatic demarche could injure the country's interest, since it could never be worse off than it was—unrecognized and unsupported by all save France. His motto was: try the experiment, we have nothing to lose. As he expressed it when opening the futile loan in February 1781: "I thought it my duty, therefore, to try the experiment, It could do no harm; for we certainly had at that moment no credit to lose." Adams, therefore, could claim that if the memorial of May 4 had done no good—and this was the opinion of Dumas—it had, nevertheless, "certainly done no harm."[59] But here, because of his ignorance of the Dutch political scene, he was mistaken. His memorial was profoundly mischievous. It was because the experienced Vauguyon immediately perceived this that he made such extraordinary exertions to talk Adams out of presenting it.

The times were even less propitious for the presentation of the May 4 memorial than they had been for the March 8 memorial. Britain had refused the Russian offer to mediate her dispute with the Dutch, presenting Catherine with the choice of defending the Dutch or abandoning them. Since the empress had never intended to permit the Armed Neutrality to drag her into a war with Britain, she decided, March 30, to let the Dutch shift for themselves. Of this decision neither the Dutch nor the British were informed until mid-May, but by late April Dutch officials began to sense that their cause was in trouble at Saint Petersburg.[60] The last thing they wanted, therefore, was an episode that would give Catherine a pretext for abandoning them. But this was precisely what Adams's memorial would furnish the czarina. It would make the Dutch appear, not as innocent neutrals pillaged by Britain but as determined enemies of George III, unable to refrain from treating with his rebel subjects. Adams's memorial, in other words, would lend a color of truth to the British claim that they had attacked the Dutch because of their settled hostility toward them. Consequently, it might allow Russia to elude her obligations to the Dutch under the Armed Neutrality.

But the memorial would do more. It would incense the British, who had never looked kindly on the sojourns of Adams and other Americans in the Netherlands. The Dutch, in their view, were giving aid and comfort to traitors; consequently, they periodically demanded that they cease harboring "the rebel subjects of his Majesty."[61] Therefore, the appearance of Adams in May at the seat of the Dutch government in the posture of a negotiator from a sovereign power was certain to inflame the British and make them implacable against the Dutch.

Adams's memorial, Vauguyon and Vergennes reasoned, would alienate the potential protector of the Dutch, Russia, while kindling the fury of Britain against them. For protection, they would have to turn to Louis XVI. Far from welcoming such a prospect, the French feared that the Dutch would conclude that, using Adams as their catspaw, they had intended to contrive just such a development. Would the Dutch, then, not recoil from such manipulation and let their inclinations lead them into the British camp? "If Holland should join England in the war, it will be unfortunate," Vauguyon warned Adams in the interviews of April 19 and 20.[62] To prevent a development so damaging to the interests of France and America, Vauguyon felt obliged to disavow Adams's actions, to convince the Dutch that he had not artfully inspired it. "I have thought," he reported to Vergennes on May 11, "to convince the preponderant members of the Republic that it had not been concerted with the ministers of the King and I have left no doubt in that regard."[63]

Vauguyon realized that his disavowal of Adams's memorial would hurt allied interests in the Netherlands. Word of his action soon leaked out. A Dutch informant of the British ministry reported on May 11, for example, that "the Ambassador of France disavows having had any notion of Adams's demarche and that he regards it as premature"; ten days later the same source reported that Vauguyon was declining to support the memorial "almost with affectation."[64] The impact of Vauguyon's repudiation of Adams was damaging because it appeared to confirm reports reaching Dutch officials from their ambassador in Paris that in the proposed Austrian–Russian mediation France had decided to forsake its commitment to the recognition of American independence.[65] Vauguyon's action, in other words, seemed to indicate that France was preparing to sacrifice the United States and end the war. Amsterdam, the center of pro-French, pro-American sentiment in the Netherlands, was dismayed by the turn of events: "The insurgents at Amsterdam," wrote a British sympathizer, "are intensely discouraged and pained."[66] Abandoned by Russia and concluding that France was in the process of disencumbering herself of the United States to make peace, the Dutch in the summer of 1781, at the initiative of Joachim Rendorp, burgomaster of Amsterdam, and other hitherto pro-French Amsterdam officials, opened negotiations with the British, through secret service agent Paul Wentworth and the Sardinian ambassador, for a separate peace. Of these negotiations and of his role in encouraging them Adams was never aware. On the contrary, he congratulated himself that "nothing but the memorial of April 19, 1781 . . . could ever have prevented this republic from making a separate peace with England."[67]

There were two more damaging consequences of Adams's memorial. In the interviews of April 19-20 Vauguyon had warned Adams of the harm the memorial would do to a loan France was trying to negotiate for the United States.[68] The ten million livres that the French had promised Franklin—and confirmed to Laurens in the spring of 1781—they proposed to obtain by borrowing in Holland. The loan was to be opened, Vergennes instructed Vauguyon on April 13, 1781, in the name of the United States, with Louis XVI guaranteeing the principal and interest.[69] But who would subscribe to a loan if the guarantor repudiated the minister of the borrower? No one, of course. France was finally obliged to change the plan of the loan and borrow in her own name with the guarantee of the States General. The money was not obtained until December 1781.[70] Finally, Vauguyon's disavowal of Adams was duly reported to Britain and undoubtedly encouraged the ministry and stiffened its opposition to the United States, now that it appeared, in Holland at least, to be in the way of being abandoned by its ally.

The Austrian-Russian mediation, which during the first half of 1781 had occupied the attention and speculation of all Europe, began to look as though it might at last materialize in May 1781. Accordingly, on May 31 Vergennes wrote the French chargé d'affaires at The Hague, Berenger (Vauguyon being on leave), instructing him to inform Adams "that the interests of the United States demand his presence here [at Paris]." Berenger sent the message to Adams at Amsterdam, but Adams refused to leave until the French gave him more information.[71] Toward the end of June, Vauguyon returned to The Hague, summoned Adams from Amsterdam, and told him that Vergennes wanted to speak to him about peace negotiations. Straightaway Adams left for Paris, arriving there on July 6.

On July 11 Vergennes revealed to him the propositions of the mediators, as they related to the United States: the gist of their proposals was that the United States and Britain negotiate separately at the mediation without any preconditions about their respective status. In the exchanges with Vergennes and with Congress which followed the disclosure of the mediators' position, Richard Morris has noted a "strange inconsistency" in Adams's conduct.[72] In fact, he conducted himself erratically, suggesting that the tension of dealing with Vergennes, the strain of the confrontation with Vauguyon, and the relentless pressure of the persecution he had been experiencing had begun to tell on him. Adams first took the position that the mediators must recognize American independence but that Britain need not. Then he shifted his ground and informed Vergennes (July 16) that neither the mediators nor Great Britain need recognize American independence in advance of a conference. Then he shifted again (July 19) and insisted that both Britain and the mediators recognize American independence in advance.[73]

Evidently perplexed, Vergennes was circumspect in answering Adams's contradictory communications. As a result, Adams assumed that the count was affecting an air of "impenetrable mystery," which lessened his confidence in him even more, if that were possible.[74] Confessing that the correspondence with Vergennes over the proposed mediation gave him "many anxious hours," Adams departed Paris on July 23 and returned to Amsterdam, where he was once more out of the count's reach.[75] In a characteristic sally, Adams later claimed that his exchanges with Vergennes had "defeated the profound and magnificent project of a congress at Vienna for the purpose of chicaning the United States out of their independence." As Bemis has pointed out, however, it was the obstinacy of George III which defeated the mediation, the British having rejected the mediators' terms on June 14, 1781, three weeks before Adams arrived in Paris to confer with Vergennes.[76]

Back in Amsterdam, Adams's world began to collapse. In the middle of August, he received a letter from Franklin at Paris, dated August 6, informing him, "I do not think we can depend on receiving any more Money here applicable to the Support of Congress Ministers." Franklin meant that he suspected that France was about to change her disbursing procedures and send her assistance directly to the Continental Congress at Philadelphia rather than funnel it through the American minister at Paris. Adams, however, jumped to the conclusion that the long-dreaded plot to starve him out had begun. On August 16 Franklin sent him dispatches from Congress containing the news that on June 13 and 14, he, Jay, Jefferson, and Laurens had been joined with him as peace negotiators.[77] The full dimensions of the plot were now clear! Having insinuated himself into the new commission, Franklin would starve him out of it and make the peace himself. Adams received Franklin's letter on the evening of August 24. The jaws of a vice, it appeared, were closing on him. The next day Adams answered the letter and then suffered what a recent biographer has called "the most severe breakdown of his life."[78]

Eighteenth-century medical terminology does not translate exactly into twentieth-century language. That Adams repeatedly described his illness as a "nervous Fever" does not mean that it was a psychological affliction. But since he himself attributed it to anxiety and since its precipitant was clearly psychogenic—the apparent crystallization of the "plot" to oust him from the peace commission—it seems safe to conclude that in August 1781 he did suffer a major nervous breakdown, accompanied by considerable somatic distress. Of the severity of the illness there can be no doubt. Adams claimed that it brought him to the "Gate of Death," that for "five or six days I was lost, and so insensible to the Operations of the Physicians and surgeons, as to have lost the memory of them." He was "still feeble" a year later, he complained.[79]

Because Adams's illness put a stop to his correspondence, we do not know when he learned the identity of those in Congress who had been responsible for the revision of his peace commission. By October 15 he knew that Congress had dropped the other shoe, by revoking (July 12) his commission to negotiate a commercial treaty with Britain, but precisely how or when he discovered this is not clear. The revision of Adams's peace commission came about in this manner. After his epistolary slugfest with Vergennes in July 1780, the count sent Luzerne, August 7, a résumé of Adams's "offenses" to enable "the ambassador to have him recalled." Not until March 1781, however, did Vergennes learn that his dispatches had miscarried and by that time he had concluded that Congress would not, in any case, recall Adams. Accordingly, Vergennes changed his strategy, instructing Luzerne on February 19, 1781, to persuade Congress to give him "a colleague capable of containing him" and on March 9 and April 19 to have Congress give Adams instructions which would "render us the masters of his conduct."[80] Having gained an extraordinary ascendancy over Congress, Luzerne produced the results that Vergennes required: on June 13-14 Congress expanded the peace commission to five and on June 15 it drafted the famous instructions ordering the commissioners to consult with the French ministry and "ultimately to govern" themselves by its advice.[81]

Adams's friends promptly wrote him of the French initiative in altering the peace commission. Vergennes, Lovell wrote on June 21, "strongly pressed" for the change.[82] Franklin's role in the proceedings was also reported to him. On July 31, 1780, Vergennes had turned his correspondence with Adams over to Franklin and requested the Doctor, in an official letter, to transmit it to Congress, so that it could judge whether Adams was "endowed . . . with that conciliatory spirit which is necessary for the important and delicate business with which he is intrusted."[83] Franklin complied with Vergennes' request and on August 9 wrote Congress a commentary on Adams's difficulties with the count. He felt obliged to do so because Vergennes appeared "much offended" with Adams and, as American representative to France, it was his duty to interpret the count's indignation for Congress. For a man whose ministerial domain Adams had repeatedly invaded, Franklin managed to be objective, stating dispassionately the difference between his and Adams's diplomatic styles—"It is my Intention . . . to procure what Advantages I can for our Country, by endeavouring to please this Court"; "Mr. Adams . . . seems to think a little apparent Stoutness, and a greater air of Independence and Boldness in our Demands, will procure us more ample Assistance"—and defending Adams as a man "who means our Welfare and Interests as much as I, or any Man, can do." Indeed, Franklin was quite solicitous about Adams, informing him, in October 1780, that he had, at Vergennes's request, transmitted his offending letters to Congress and inviting him "to write something for effacing the Impression made by them," an invitation that Adams ignored.[84]

In the course of the congressional debate about restructuring the peace commission, Vergennes's letter to Franklin of July 31 and Franklin's to Congress of August 9 became objects of consideration. Copies of the letters were transmitted to Adams, who received Franklin's at least by December 2, 1781, probably much earlier.[85] The interpretation that Adams gave Franklin's letter was predictable: it was an "assassination upon my Character," produced by "base Jealousy" and "sordid Envy." "Jealousy and envy," Adams asserted, "engender[ed] malice and revenge," which would only cease when Franklin obtained his long standing goal of driving him out of Europe.[86] If the revision of the peace commission had a positive aspect for Adams, it was this: he now had what he considered to be incontestable "proof," in the form of copies of Franklin's and Vergennes's letters, that the two were conspiring to persecute him.

As Adams pulled out of the depths of his breakdown, he began to confront some of the problems that had overtaken him. Writing Franklin on October 4, 1781, he declared, "If you refuse to pay my subsistence, I shall have no recourse but to return to America." "The moment you take the resolution to refuse payment of my salary" would you "apply to his excellency the Marquis De Castries and ask the favor of a passage for me, on board the first king's ship to America?" Otherwise, Adams must take his chances aboard a merchantman. "It would be a gloomy lot to me," he continued, "to be taken prisoner by the English. They would treat me with a contempt and insolence, beyond any which they have yet marked to any of their prisoners. They have ancient as well as modern grudges against me, which every body in the world does not know or suspect as yet." But, Adams concluded, "I had infinitely rather suffer the consequences of their malice and revenge and lie in the Tower or in Newgate, weak, infirm or sick as I am" than go around Holland begging for subsistence. A bit more reflection convinced Adams that he should ask Congress for his recall, which he did on October 15.[87] But he finally decided to put the best face he could on affairs and stay on a while in the Netherlands, reduced though he was "to a miserable state of health by anxiety of mind . . . menaced with an axe and hurdle in London, threatened with starvation from Passy; and having frequently suggested to my recollection, the butcher's knife, with which the De Witts had been cut up at the Hague."[88]

CHAPTER 5

DUTCH RECOGNITION

In the fall of 1781 changes occurred in Dutch politics. On September 7, 1781, the British cabinet accepted a new Russian offer to mediate the conflict with the Netherlands. Galitzin, the Russian ambassador at The Hague, announced the British decision to the States General on November 9. "A new order of things had developed," Vauguyon declared, for whether by accident or design the alteration in British policy coincided with a significant realignment of Dutch political forces. From the beginning of Anglo-Dutch hostilities Amsterdam had been the soul of the struggle against Great Britain. But in the fall of 1781 what Vauguyon described as a "great number" of Amsterdam magistrates, led by the burgomaster Rendorp, who had conducted the secret peace negotiations with Britain in July and August, sought a reconciliation with the stadtholder and his party.[1] The rapprochement of "Messers d'Amsterdam" with the passionately pro-British stadtholder, at the moment Britain accepted the Russian mediation, alarmed Vergennes. Were the Dutch about to conclude a dishonorable peace with Britain at France's expense?[2] Even if they refused to appease the British, the Dutch, by concluding a precipitate peace, would damage France. The arrival in Europe at the end of November 1781 of the news of the decisive Franco-American victory at Yorktown opened the prospect that Britain might be compelled to sue for peace. It was in France's interest that a peace negotiation be general—that all the enemies of Britain negotiate with her concurrently. Vergennes feared that the British might try for quick settlements with the Netherlands and the United States—North and Fox explored these avenues in March and April 1782[3]—in order to intensify the war against France to obtain better terms from her. Therefore, he ordered Vauguyon to exert himself to prevent the Dutch from concluding a separate peace with the British; "the French Ambassador," reported a British emissary in Holland, "was sedulous to retard the negotiation of Peace."[4]

Also opposed to composing the quarrel with Britain were the former associates of Amsterdam in the anti-British opposition; led by the magistrates of Dort, they found their strength in the smaller cities of Holland such as Leyden, Haerlem, and Alcmaer, and in the province of Friesland.[5] These men wanted to reform the Dutch government by increasing the power of the people at the expense of the power of the stadtholder. Their cause flourished as long as the high-handed hostility of Britain discredited the stadtholder and his supporters. They feared, however, that if the stadtholder and his new allies at Amsterdam succeeded in negotiating an honorable peace with Britain, the old oligarchy would regain its credit and the possibility of democratic reform would disappear.[6] Therefore, the "zealous patriots," as Vauguyon called them, shared the interest of France in preventing a Dutch-British rapprochement and joined with Vauguyon to obstruct it.

What was the best means to keep the Dutch and British apart? An offensive and defensive alliance with France would do it, but although many zealous patriots urged the conclusion of such a compact, the majority preferred something short of binding ties to Louis XVI. France, moreover, did not want to be bound by an alliance with the Dutch. But what if the Dutch recognized American independence? Such an act would bind no one in an unwanted alliance, yet it would exasperate Britain to a degree that would destroy any possibility of an accommodation with the

Netherlands. It would "have the essential effect in their [the zealous patriots'] eyes of rendering impossible the rapprochement of the Republic and England." It would, declared Vauguyon, be "the surest means of breaking forever the ties between the Republic and England."[7] Therefore, in the aftermath of British acceptance of Russian mediation, Vauguyon and the Dutch patriot faction, for reasons having nothing to do with Adams's efforts in the Netherlands, vigorously pursued the goal of procuring a Dutch recognition of American independence.

In the middle of December 1781, for example, the "most zealous members of several provinces came to explain themselves" to Vauguyon "in a manner the most energetic on the necessity of a union with the 13 United States of America." Perplexed about how to bring the American question into the public eye, Vauguyon's visitors accepted his suggestion that the corpse of Adams's memorial of May 4, 1781, lying lifeless in a clerk's office at The Hague, be revived. Adams, the duke advised, should be encouraged to go to the States General and "demand of the president of the week if the mémoire which he had previously submitted . . . had been the object of their deliberations and to press them to give him a response."[8] The zealous patriots agreed, invited Adams to The Hague, and urged him to take the step. Vauguyon went to Amsterdam, where he pressed the same action on Adams. "He thinks," Adams reported to Congress, "that I may now assume a higher tone, which the late *Cornwallization* will well warrant." Accordingly, on January 9, 1782, Adams went to the president and demanded a categorical answer about the fate of his memorial of May 4, 1781.[9] What, he asked, had the States General done about his request that it conclude a treaty of amity and commerce with the United States? The president reported Adams's inquiry to the States General, thus bringing the question of relations with the United States before that body and enabling members from individual provinces to refer it back to their constituents. In this way was the possibility of recognizing American independence, at the beginning of 1782, made a subject of political debate in the public forums of the Netherlands.

British peace initiatives soon prompted the proponents of American independence to redouble their efforts. In response to the "earnest sollicitation" of Rendorp and his Amsterdam colleagues in December 1781 and pursuant to Britain's own desires for a "cordial Reconciliation" with the Dutch, the British ministry in January 1782 dispatched Paul Wentworth, who had conferred confidentially with Rendorp in the summer of 1781, to the Netherlands to conduct another secret negotiation. Wentworth's "ostensible commission"—his cover, as Lord Stormont called it—was to negotiate an exchange of prisoners. His real mission was "to endeavor to *preparer les Voies* by settling such Preliminaries as may form the Basis of a Definitive Treaty, to be concluded . . . under the Mediation of the Empress of Russia." Wentworth arrived at The Hague on February 1, 1782, and immediately began negotiations with van der Hoop, an official of the Amsterdam Admiralty, who had been selected to conduct the secret talks by the stadtholder, the grand pensionary of Holland, and Rendorp, by the leaders, in other words, of the Orangist-Amsterdam coalition. Vauguyon, who returned to the Netherlands on February 6 after a seven-week stay in France, was immediately informed of Wentworth's mission and mobilized his resources to counteract it.[10]

In the diplomatic duel that followed, conducted largely out of the public eye, Vauguyon held all the cards. When Britain commenced hostilities against the Dutch in December 1780, the decrepitude of the Dutch military establishment forced the Dutch East India Company to seek French protection. In the spring of 1781 France began convoying the company's ships. By the time Wentworth arrived in Holland France had, moreover, sent 2,000 men to protect the East India Company's valuable colony at the Cape of Good Hope and 1,200 men to Ceylon. These arrangements, Rendorp remarked to Wentworth, made the East India Company "more dependent on France than on Holland." But

Dutch obligations to France did not stop here. Between November 1781 and January 1782 France captured from the British the Dutch colonies of Saint Eustatia, Demarara, and Essequibo; she would restore them, it was presumed, at the end of the war if the Dutch continued to act in a friendly manner. Finally, the Dutch land forces, which had not escaped the decay of the country's military establishment, could offer no resistance to an invading French army. "They are in bodily fear of a hundred thousand men from France," Adams declared. France had, Vauguyon boasted to Vergennes, "the means on all sides to annihilate the republic" and, although the duke did not try to arouse Dutch fears, everyone in the Netherlands was aware of his country's vulnerability. We are "at the Mercy of France," van der Hoop confessed to Wentworth.[11]

Having accurately assessed their situation, the Dutch, as van der Hoop admitted to Wentworth, knew that "it was out of their Power to make a peace which should not have . . . the approbation of France." On February 18 van der Hoop sought Vauguyon's blessing for negotiations with the British, assuming, he informed the duke, that France "would see without pain the Republic terminate the war by obtaining recognition the most unlimited of their neutral rights."[12]

By insisting on "unlimited" rights, the Dutch assured the failure of the negotiation with Wentworth, for he had been instructed to insist, as a sine qua non, on a revision of the treaty of 1674 to prevent future Dutch carriage of naval stores to France in wartime. Not being privy to Wentworth's instructions, Vauguyon did not know that there were irreconcilable differences over what Stormont called the "perpetual stumbling Block" of the carriage of naval stores in wartime. Rather, Vauguyon feared that Britain might make peace by capitulating to Dutch demands.[13] The duke, therefore, sought to prevent an accommodation—by precipitating, if possible, a Dutch recognition of American independence. To this end, Vauguyon and his allies, the zealous patriots, bent their efforts in February 1782.

Vauguyon had extended his relations in the Netherlands as widely as possible, he reported to Vergennes on December 11, 1781; he had "intimate liaisons with several magistrates of the different cities of Holland as well as with several members of the provinces." He now mobilized his supporters across the country, causing van der Hoop to complain to Wentworth, February 23, 1782, about the "Spirit of the People" having "become turbulent by the Machinations of the French Ambassador and adherents of the French Interest." The firstfruits of these "machinations" were in Friesland, long a hotbed of French influence. On February 26 Friesland became, as Adams put it, "the second sovereign state in Europe" to acknowledge American independence.[14] At the same time the province of Holland began moving toward a recognition of American independence. On February 22 it considered Adams's demand of January 9 and the next day adjourned until March 6, charging its members to examine Adams's demand and "to return . . . with their opinions on the subject."[15] To rally public opinion and put pressure on the provincial delegates, the zealous patriots in the various cities of Holland prepared petitions in support of American independence and encouraged merchants to sign them. Throughout the province and in Amsterdam itself merchants presented themselves "in crowds" to subscribe their names.[16]

The warming of Amsterdam to American independence was the result of an impasse in negotiations with Wentworth. By mid-March it was apparent to Rendorp and his associates that an agreement was impossible; on March 12, therefore, van Bleiswyck, the grand pensionary of Holland, presented Wentworth an ultimatum, demanding that he accede to Dutch terms or return to England. Wentworth attempted to spin negotiations out, but on March 18, at a secret, "extraordinary Town Council" meeting in Amsterdam, a resolution was passed, recognizing American independence. Wentworth's presence in the Netherlands was now untenable and he left the country on March 21, signaling the victory of France and her Dutch adherents over those of their countrymen who wanted a reconciliation with Britain.[17]

Since the other cities in Holland were ardently pro-French, pro-American independence, the decision of Amsterdam to join them meant that recognition of the United States by the province was assured. On March 28 Holland voted without dissent for recognition. "The unanimous desire of the province of Holland so energetically pronounced," Vauguyon wrote Vergennes on March 29, "has entirely established the national sentiment."[18] The duke was correct, for the remaining provinces of the confederation quickly fell in behind Holland and Friesland, to whom they had agreed to defer, as being the leading maritime provinces and, hence, as Guelderland put it, "the most interested in the decision in that affair."[19] During the first part of April the provinces recognized American independence one after another. On April 19 the States General officially declared that, since all seven provinces had consented, the United States of America was acknowledged to be a sovereign nation and that Adams was admitted as minister plenipotentiary. Vauguyon, reported a Dutch observer, gave "a great ministerial dinner to celebrate the said admission, for which he had worked with zeal and much eagerness (beaucoup d'empressement)."[20]

What was Adams's role in the rush of events leading to the recognition of American independence? He can best be compared to a man on a raft, being borne toward his objective by powerful but imperceptible currents. Adams was deeply ignorant about what was happening in Holland in the winter of 1782. His illness was partly to blame. He was weak and lame, he reported on December 26, 1781; his health was "precarious," he wrote on February 14, 1782; he was "so feeble that it fatigues me more to write one letter than it did ten when we were together at Paris," he wrote Dana on March 15.[21] The result was that he did not have the energy to get around and inform himself about what was happening. His debility deepened the information gap caused by his isolation from mainstream Dutch politicians, who, in the winter of 1782, were still avoiding him like a "pestilence." Having shifted to a pro-British orientation, the Amsterdam politicians, in fact, put more distance between themselves and Adams than ever before. Consequently, on January 14, 1782, Adams made the remarkable confession that having lived in Amsterdam for eighteen months, he was "a stranger to the great city and the characters that govern it."[22]

How little Adams knew about what was going on in Holland in the winter of 1782 can be demonstrated by his virtual ignorance of the crucial Wentworth negotiations. He knew that Amsterdam had "visibly altered its sentiments" and he knew that some sort of "secret intrigues" were going on. Rendorp, he suspected, was involved and Dumas wrote from The Hague that "l'Emissaire Wentworth" was up to something. But Adams seems to have known nothing about Wentworth's real business, his only statement about him being the characteristic one that he had "come over to watch" him.[23]

Adams knew as little about Vauguyon's activities as he did of Wentworth's. His estrangement from the duke continued until he moved to The Hague in May 1782. Some communication occurred during the crucial months of 1782, but it was minimal. Adams, therefore, could judge Vauguyon's activities only by what he saw of them in public. In 1782, however, the duke was deliberately keeping the lowest possible public profile, for at Vergennes's repeated directions he was still pursuing the policy of "circumspection" which he had followed since Adams had been in Holland. This was especially true with respect to his strenuous efforts to produce a Dutch acknowledgment of American independence, a step fraught with danger for the Dutch and one that France, therefore, did not want "to impose upon ourselves the obligation of guaranteeing the consequences." Accordingly, Vauguyon scrupulously refrained from publicly pressuring the Dutch into supporting American independence. "I am so dedicated to the circumspection and reserve which you have recommended to me," he wrote Vergennes on March 20 "that whatever may be the fate of that great event the Dutch will never be able to attribute it to our entreaties."[24] Adams, certainly, did not attribute any Dutch actions to Vauguyon's entreaties. In the recognition of American independence, he wrote Franklin on March 26, Vauguyon had not been visible, had not done "any ministerial act," and therefore, concluded Adams, he had not done anything at all.[25]

Adams, in fact, persisted in believing that French diplomacy was the principal obstacle to the American cause in the Netherlands. To William Gordon on April 15, 1783, he wrote: "The finesse and subtilty of the 2 ministers [Vergennes and Vauguyon] were exhausted to defeat me, by disgusting and discouraging me, by Neglects, Slights, Contempts, Attacks & Maneuvers, & every thing but an avowed open opposition."[26] Repeating the charge later, Adams claimed that "in proportion as the probability of my obtaining the object [recognition] so long pursued increased my disguised enemies redoubled their secret intrigues . . . the comte Vergennes was certainly mortified at my prospects of success."[27] In fact, on April 27, 1782, Vergennes congratulated Vauguyon on the realization of France's long-standing goal of a "coalition between the two republics," as he had described it on February 19, 1781.[28] Adams's admission as minister plenipotentiary "could not be more important in the actual conjunction," Vergennes wrote, for "it is an invincible obstacle to the actual reconciliation of England and Holland."[29]

Adams's conviction of French malevolence made it easier for him to exaggerate the importance of his own activities, for had he known, or even suspected, the nature of Vauguyon's efforts on behalf of American independence, he would not have assumed, as he did, that Dutch recognition was entirely owing to his own exertions. As it was, Adams talked of "my success in Holland as the happiest Event, and the greatest Action of my Life past or future."[30] His assessment of his "success" was generous indeed. The Dutch negotiation, he declared, "accelerated the peace, more than the capture of Cornwallis and his whole army"; it was more decisive "than any battle or siege, by land or Sea, during the entire war"; it "produced" the British acknowledgment of American independence and the handsome peace terms won at Paris in the fall of 1782.[31]

Is there any substance to these claims? No historian supports them. In fact, the relation of the British and Dutch recognition of American independence appears to be exactly the reverse of that described by Adams. Dutch recognition was expedited by the resolution passed by the British Parliament, reeling from Yorktown, on February 27, 1782, declaring advocates of "offensive war in America" enemies of their country and authorizing the king to make peace with the "revolted colonies of North America."[32] Wrote Vauguyon to Vergennes on March 5: "The important scene which the British Parliament has offered the 27th of last month . . . could contribute, M le Comte, to hasten the resolution of the States General on the recognition of American independence. In effect, it has appeared to them probably dangerous to elude the advances of Congress in a moment when it seems to be regarded as independent by England itself." Wrote Wentworth to Stormont two days later: "The measures proposed by the opposition in Parliament hasten the Idea of American independence and induce proposals here, untho't of before—it may precipitate Mr. Adams' reception." Finally, there is the testimony of Rendorp to Wentworth on March 22: "We ought always to listen to Adams to know what he proposes: your parliament sets us the example."[33] Dutch recognition of American independence, far from precipitating a similar action by the British, was, in fact, produced by events in Parliament.

Immediately after being received as minister plenipotentiary, Adams presented Dutch officials a project of a treaty of amity and commerce. Although it soon became apparent that the Dutch and he agreed on the principal points of the treaty, the complexities of the Dutch government, which required that proposals be filtered through several layers of officials and, in the case of a marine treaty, through different boards of admiralty, and the captiousness of some Dutch negotiators delayed the conclusion of a treaty until October 8.[34] It would not have been completed then had it not been for Vauguyon. "The perfection of that work," wrote a well-informed Dutchman "ought to be attributed to the care of the Duke de la Vauguyon, who in his daily conferences with the ministers much insisted on it."[35]

Adams was less interested in concluding the commercial treaty than he was in discharging a commission that Congress had given him on August 16, 1781. A resolution that accompanied the commission explained that in response to an offer from France—to "the tender of [Louis XVI's] endeavors to accomplish a coalition between the United Provinces of the Netherlands and these States"—Adams was instructed to propose a triple alliance between France, the Netherlands, and the United States, including Spain as a fourth partner, if she wanted to join.[36] Since he believed that "a quadruple alliance for the duration of the war would probably soon bring it to a conclusion," Adams assigned top priority to negotiating it.

The commission of August 16 demonstrates how badly Adams and his colleagues were often served by Congress in foreign affairs. Adams assumed that he had inspired the French demarche at Philadelphia which produced the commission. To Robert Livingston on February 21, 1782, he explained that he had written Vauguyon on May 1, 1781, proposing an alliance between France, the Netherlands, and the United States. "The Duke," he continued, "transmitted the letter to the Count de Vergennes, which produced the offer to Congress from the King, to assist us in forming a connection with the republic."[37] In fact, the offer of French good offices to Congress was conveyed by Vergennes to Luzerne in a dispatch of February 19, 1781. [38] On July 20 Luzerne informed a committee of Congress of France's willingness to promote a Dutch-American coalition. The committee reported the minister's offer to the full Congress on July 23, in terms which showed that it had not misunderstood its limits: Congress should prepare "the means of uniting the interest of the two republicks by making proper advances to the States General. The minister added that he was authorized by the king to offer Congress his interposition for this purpose."[39] In drafting instructions for Adams on August 16, Congress unilaterally transformed France's offer of good offices into orders to Adams to propose a triple alliance between France, the Netherlands, and the United States. A more irresponsible mandate can scarcely be imagined. Nations simply do not order their representatives to propose alliances between other nations who have expressed no interest in them.

In transmitting an account of the August 16 instructions to Vergennes, Luzerne admitted that he had not superintended their drafting with his customary vigilance: "I had no manner of influence on that resolution," he wrote the count. Nor did he deny that the instructions were "far from the overtures I had made to Congress." When Vergennes received the instructions, he was incensed by Congress's presumption in ordering Adams to propose an alliance between France and the Netherlands. Congress had been "careless," he complained; its instructions were, in fact, a "Résolution défiante." Accordingly, he ordered Vauguyon to oppose any attempt Adams made to negotiate a triple alliance, counsel that Vauguyon, who was astonished that a third party would presume to "propose to the States General a coalition with his Majesty," did not need.[40] The effect on Adams can easily be imagined. Each time he attempted to obey his instructions (November 1781, March 1782), drawn apparently at France's instigation, he was rebuffed by France. Nothing could have been better calculated to reinforce his conviction of French malevolence toward the United States and toward him personally.

Adams's bitterness toward France revealed itself in the spring of 1782 by the manner in which he negotiated a loan with the Dutch, the States General's recognition of American independence having finally made overtures to the Amsterdam financial community feasible. Franklin and Vergennes recommended that

Adams open a loan with the French government's bankers in the Netherlands, Fizeau and Grand, one of whose partners, George Grand, was a close friend of Vergennes. Adams refused because he feared that Fizeau and Grand "would furnish Versailles and Passy with information of every guilder I might from time to time obtain; and I had seen enough of the intrigues and waste from that quarter, to be determined at all risques not to open a loan in that house singly." As if to spite the French, Adams opened his loan on May 1 with John Hodshon and Son, well-known partisans of England. That this move was ill advised Adams himself later admitted, for a "clamour arouse upon change in the city and pretty extensively in various parts of the republic" against Hodshon because of his rabid "Anglomania." Adams, it was incredulously charged, had selected a banker who was "an enemy to America." Consequently, on May 3 he was forced to suspend the loan.[41] He reopened it successfully at a later date with a consortium of Dutch bankers.

In the middle of June Adams again pressed Vauguyon to support him in implementing the August 16 commission. Adams believed, wrote Vauguyon to Vergennes on June 17, 1782, "that when the treaty of commerce which he had proposed shall be concluded, it would be useful and even necessary for him to make a new démarche to the States General and invite them to adhere to the treaty of alliance between His Majesty and the United States." Rein Adams in, Vergennes instructed Vauguyon on June 23; let him "limit himself, for the present, to his treaty of commerce."[42]

Adams approached Vauguyon again in the middle of July. The province of Holland was about to approve the commercial treaty, he declared. Therefore he concluded that the time had come to propose the triple alliance; since Vauguyon was "not positively charged to forbid him to execute his project he believed himself obliged to persist in it." Vergennes now took a higher tone and ordered Adams, through Vauguyon, to communicate his project to France and not proceed with it "without having the sentiments of the King beforehand." On August 16 Vauguyon reported that he believed that he had talked Adams out of proposing the triple alliance. A decisive interview took place on August 18, at which Adams agreed to submit the triple alliance project to Vergennes and renounce it, if the count disapproved. That Vergennes would disapprove Vauguyon left Adams little doubt.[43]

August 18 was a bad day for Adams. Not only was he thwarted by the French but the shadow of Franklin fell across his path. On the eighteenth Adams obtained a copy of the commission of Alleyne Fitzherbert, the British diplomat who had been sent to Paris to negotiate with the French. Fitzherbert's commission contained an equivocal reference to the United States, which aroused Adams's fury against Franklin. Adams had picked up rumors of a trip to London by one of the Doctor's cronies, William Alexander, in which Alexander was alleged to have informed the British ministry that an acknowledgment of American independence was not a sine qua non in the peace negotiations which were under way in the summer of 1782. Fitzherbert's commission was, in Adams's mind, the result of Alexander's trip, for which Franklin was obviously responsible.

Far from sanctioning Alexander's mission, Franklin was barely aware of it.[44] But Adams considered the mission as evidence that the Doctor was monopolizing and mismanaging the peace negotiations. He had not, he wrote Congress on April 18, "refused to act in the commission with him [Franklin], because I thought it possible that I might perhaps do some little good in it and prevent some evil."[45] But evil, evidently, was going to prevail and, as Adams reflected on being impeded by Vergennes and overreached by Franklin, his prospects at the peace table appeared dim indeed. "Knowing that I should have the Count and the Doctor to combat almost in every step of the negotiation for peace," he wrote, "I thought I should be useless and my situation very unpleasant. This prospect staggered my fortitude for a moment and I thought of resigning."[46] And, in fact, Adams did offer his resignation in his letter of August 18, but, as on earlier occasions, he retracted it and resolved to stay on in Europe for a while longer. On September 28 John Jay wrote him that Britain had at last acknowledged American independence, by agreeing to treat with "the Commissioners of the United States of America."[47] Come to Paris and join the negotiations, Jay urged him. Jay's invitation was too pressing to refuse. In mid-October Adams left The Hague and set off for Paris, resolved to endure whatever trials awaited him in the French capital.

CHAPTER 6

PEACE NEGOTIATIONS

Adams arrived in Paris on October 26, 1782, and prepared for
the peace negotiations by outfitting himself, from wig to shoes,
in French fashions and by taking a bath in the Seine. The waters
cleansed the outer man only, however; they did not wash away
Adams's apprehensions about Franklin and Vergennes.

The revocation of his commission as sole peace negotiator had,
he wrote Dana on December 14, 1781, "removed the cause of
envy, I had like to have said, but I fear I must retract since JA
still stands before BF in the commission." Throughout 1782 he
was convinced that Franklin's envy was doing its dirty work. He
assumed, he wrote Robert Livingston on February 21, 1782, that
the Doctor was writing Congress, charging him with excessive
vanity. Nor did he doubt that Franklin was deprecating his
Dutch mission. His success in Holland would be represented as a
"Thing of Course, and of little Consequence," he wrote his wife
on May 14. "Jealousy is as cruel as the Grave, and Envy as spight-
full as Hell." "The Malice with which those whom he [Franklin]
dislikes are pursued" is incredible, Adams wrote Edmund Jenings on August 12.[1]

"Contempt and Abhorrence" for Franklin was the attitude
Adams brought to Paris and it produced the following scene a
few days after his arrival. Matthew Ridley, deputed by Maryland
to borrow money in Europe, visited Adams on October 29 and

reminded him that courtesy required that he call on Franklin. "There was no necessity," Adams exploded. "After the usage he had received from him he could not bear to go near him. . . . He said the D[octor] might come to him. I [Ridley] told him that . . . the last comer always paid the first visit. He replied the Dr. was to come to him. he was first in the Comm[issio]n. I ask[ed] him how the D was to know he was here unless he went to him. He replied that was true, he did not think of that and would go. Afterwards when pulling on his Coat he said he would not, he could not bear to go where the D. was. With much persuasion I got him at length to go."[2]

Adams was no better disposed toward Vergennes, smarting as he was from what he believed to be the count's obstructions of his efforts in the Netherlands. He had "ten thousand reasons," he wrote Livingston on September 6, to believe that Vergennes had "not wished that we should form connections with Holland, even as soon as we did, or with any other power." Vergennes, Adams complained to Jonathan Jackson on November 17, had attempted to undermine him in Holland by instructing Vauguyon "to prevent if possible our Success. . . . I declare that he did every Thing in his Power to prevent me." The angry exchanges with Vergennes in the summer of 1780 and the contentious interviews in the summer of 1781 were still fresh in Adams's mind. If he called on the count, would he hear an "expostulation? a reproof? an admonition? or in plain vulgar English, a Scolding?" To spare himself a scene, Adams avoided Vergennes. He was in Paris a full two weeks before the count discovered "from the Returns of the Police" that he was in town.[3]

And then there was John Jay, the other principal in the negotiations with the British. Adams and Jay had been political opponents in the Continental Congress, disagreeing frequently and "with ardour." The two men had been, as Adams put it, members of "different sects." Since Jay's fellow communicants were Silas Deane and men of his stripe, Adams "concluded that Mr. Jay would concur with Dr. Franklin and make a majority against me." On the other hand, Adams had received intimations in Holland that Jay was at odds with Franklin, intelligence that Ridley confirmed on October 27. Jay had been standing out against both Franklin and Vergennes, Ridley reported. "R[idley] is full of Js Firmness and Independence," Adams noted in his diary.[4]

On October 28 Adams met Jay and listened for three hours to his "conjectures as to the views of France and Spain."[5] We can be sure that what he heard did no honor to the House of Bourbon. During the summer of 1782 Jay had conducted a desultory negotiation with the Spanish ambassador at Versailles, the Count de Aranda, about the western boundary between the United States and Spain. Aranda had claimed most of the Old Northwest and Southwest for Charles III, while Jay had doggedly insisted that the Mississippi River was the western boundary of the United States. When the negotiations reached an impasse, Aranda appealed to Vergennes for support. The count delegated his secretary, Gérard de Rayneval, to confer with Aranda, and together the two men concocted a scheme that would have given the lands south of the Ohio River to Spain, those north of it to Great Britain.[6] Rayneval embodied these proposals in a memoir and presented it to Jay on September 6, taking care to preserve the fiction that the paper contained his personal ideas only. Four days later the British handed the American minister a dispatch, written by Luzerne's secretary, Barbé-Marbois, which argued that France was under no obligation to support American claims to fishing rights on the banks of Newfoundland. On October 24 Rayneval treated Jay to another disquisition against the extravagance of American land claims, and contested, as had Marbois, the "propriety" of American fishing pretentions.[7]

Jay suspected that, having found him obdurate, the French had carried their case against the United States directly to the British. Rayneval had gone off to London immediately after presenting his memoir of September 6 and Jay persuaded himself that he had been sent by Vergennes to tell Shelburne that France did not countenance her ally's demands and that she would welcome British opposition to them. Jay's conjectures about France's policy Adams summarized as follows: "Our Allies dont play us fair, he told me. They were endeavouring to deprive Us of the Fishery, the Western Lands, and the Navigation of the Mississippi. They would even bargain with the English to deprive us of them."[8]

Adams agreed with Jay's conclusions—we are in danger of being "duped out of the fishery, the Mississippi, much of the western lands," he informed Livingston on November 8[9]—because they fit his conviction that France was trying to keep the United States weak and dependent upon her. But Adams, as usual, misjudged what France was doing. While it was true that Spain's claims to the American West contravened the interests of the United States, France was supporting them not to injure America but to maintain loyalty to her Bourbon neighbor, her partner in the Family Compact and therefore her primary ally. This, however, was not the way Adams saw it. He assumed that France was advocating the Spanish claim "to plant the Seeds of Contention for a future War." "Knowing the fine Country in the Neighbourhood, and the rapidity with which it would fill with Inhabitants," France, Adams conjectured, foresaw that Americans would tolerate no restraints from Spain but would "force their way down the Mississipi and occasion another War . . . in which we should stand in need of France."[10] If France's policy had actually been based on the motives Adams attributed to it, she would have been striving to pit her oldest and best ally against her newest and most uncertain one, provoking a war between the two nations in which she would support the United States and alienate (and possibly be at war with) her far more valuable friend, Spain. French policy was not, of course, so irrational and self-destructive.

Adams assumed that France, by refusing to support American fishing claims, was attempting to embroil the United States in a war in another part of North America. France's position on the fisheries—like her support of Spain's claims in the American West—was contrary to American interests, but it was not malicious. The Treaty of Paris of 1763 had assigned France the right to dry fish at Newfoundland, but the British immediately began encroaching on the territory reserved for the French. Violence resulted and in 1775 Britain paid France a large indemnity for assaults on her fishermen. In that and the following year Vergennes negotiated strenuously with Lords Rochford and Weymouth for confirmation of exclusive French fishing and drying rights in Newfoundland.[11] When France, therefore, pressed Britain in 1782 for exclusive fishing rights, secured against both British and American encroachments, and at the same time attempted to dissuade the Americans from pushing their fishing claims to their fullest extent, she was pursuing a policy defined years earlier, not inventing means to weaken the United States. But Adams saw it differently. Britain might fall in with French proposals to limit American fishing rights in Newfoundland, but the New England fishermen, "the boldest Men alive," would not relinquish their hereditary haunts. In trying to keep them out of Newfoundland waters, the British might, Adams conceded, sink "now and then a fishing Schooner but this would not prevent a repetition of the crime, it would only inflame and irritate and inkindle a New War," in which the United States would be forced to depend on France.[12]

Every move France made during the peace negotiations Adams interpreted as aspects of the plot to make America dependent. In a conversation of November 10, 1782, Vergennes sympathized with the British demand that the United States compensate the Tories. "All the precedents were in their favor," the count observed, "there never had been an example of such an affair terminated by treaty, but all were restored."[13] Why had France become "advocates of the Tories"? Adams knew. If reintroduced into American society, the Tories "would contribute to perpetual alienation against England" and would be used by "French emissaries" to "blow up the flames of Animosity and

War" between Britain and America, in which the United States would, of course, be forced to depend upon France.

During the peace negotiations, Britain refused to restore commerce with the United States to its prewar footing. France was responsible for British recalcitrance, Adams believed. In causing the revocation of his commission to negotiate a commercial treaty with Britain—as Adams assumed that Vergennes had—the French meant "to dampen the Ardor of returning Friendship" by embroiling Britain and the United States in a commercial dispute. To advance the scheme, France had, Adams concluded, planted emissaries at the Court of St. James's who persuaded the British ministry to issue the famous order-in-council of July 2, 1783, excluding American shipping from British West Indian ports. Adams firmly believed that this celebrated measure, which pointed a dagger at the heart of American commerce, was adopted upon the "advice and desire" of France.[14]

Adams's conviction that France wanted to keep the United States dependent upon her proceeded inexorably from the summer of 1780 onward, furnishing the interpretation for every French action he encountered. As an interpretation of specific actions, whether of France's failure to establish naval superiority on the American coastline in 1780, of France's policy toward the United States in the Netherlands in 1781 and 1782, or of French "instigation" of the British order-in-council of July 2, 1783, it was always wrong. But the paradox is that if the conviction was wrong in its parts, it was correct overall. It was as if a column of errors had been added together and produced a truth. France actually did want to keep America dependent upon her after the war's end. But the means by which she aspired to do this—leaving Canada in British hands—Adams never suspected.[15]

However reached, Adams's conclusion was valuable because French and American interests were in conflict at many points during the peace negotiations of 1782 and the United States would have suffered had its negotiators assumed undiluted French benevolence toward their country. It was Samuel F.

Bemis's thesis that the diplomacy of the Revolution demonstrated how the United States obtained advantages from Europe's distresses. In Adams's case the United States obtained advantages from conclusions produced by its own servant's distresses.

Not the least of the advantages of Adams's suspicion of France was that it positioned him to join Franklin and Jay in flouting Congress's instruction of June 15, 1781, which enjoined the peace commissioners "to make the most candid and confidential communications upon all subjects to the ministers of our generous ally . . . and ultimately to govern yourself by their advice and opinion."[16] Jay had ignored the instruction from the beginning of the negotiations with the British. Franklin appeared more equivocal about disregarding it (although in fact his disobedience to it preceded Jay's). Adams's contempt for the instruction—he compared it to the Declaratory Act of 1766 in the way that the French "had been given Jurisdiction over us in all cases whatsoever"—assured that the American negotiators would scorn it. On October 30, at the first meeting of the enlarged American commission with a reinforced team of British negotiators, Franklin pronounced its epitaph by turning to Jay and declaring: "I am of your Opinion and will go on with these Gentlemen in the Business without consulting this Court."[17] With Adams bolstering his colleagues' defiance, there was no chance that the American negotiators would allow themselves to be imposed upon by France.

When the American commissioners met British negotiator Richard Oswald and his new colleague, Henry Strachey, on October 30, the status of the negotiations was as follows: on October 5 Jay, whom Adams later extolled as the "principal negotiator" of the peace,[18] had persuaded the pliant Oswald to initial a set of articles that fixed the United States' southern boundary at "the 31°—St. Mary's River line," its western boundary at the Mississippi River, and its northern boundary at the so-called Nipissing Line (which included the southern part of the province of Ontario); the boundary between Nova Scotia and Maine was to be referred to the adjudication of a joint commission; Americans were to have the "Right to take Fish of every kind on the Banks of Newfoundland and other places where the Inhabitants of both Countries used formerly . . . also to dry and Cure the same at the accustomed Places."[19] No provisions were made for the payment of British debts that Americans had contracted before the war, nor were the Tories to be compensated for their losses.

Jay made two concessions in negotiating these preliminaries that ultimately cost the Commonwealth of Massachusetts. In a draft that he handed Oswald on October 5, he contended for the Saint John River as the boundary between the United States and Nova Scotia. When Oswald objected, Jay expressed a willingness "to set that Matter to rights, so as the Massachusetts Government shall have no more of that Coast than they had before the War." He had, he admitted, taken his directions from maps which were "not distinct" and which did not agree, and, therefore, he consented to include in the preliminaries sent to London an article referring the northeast boundary to future adjudication. Jay's pliancy on this point evidently encouraged the British cabinet to instruct Strachey to try to push the Maine boundary as far south as the Sagadahoc (Androscoggin) River or, failing this, at least to the Penobscot. It did not, however, make either of these lines an ultimatum and would, apparently, have conceded the Saint John River boundary. When Adams joined the negotiations, he tried to insist that the Saint John was the true northeastern boundary.[20] Had he, rather than Jay, conducted the negotiations leading to the draft of October 5, the United States might well have gotten the Saint John River as its northeastern boundary and a boundary dispute that festered for half a century might have been prevented.

Jay's second concession concerned fish. He had, in the draft of October 5, claimed for his countrymen a right to dry fish on the shores of Newfoundland. Franklin had not included this claim in his "necessary" articles of July 10, 1782, which the British were using as a guideline in the negotiations.[21] Oswald suspected, however, that the Doctor's assertion of fishing rights comprehended drying rights as well. When he queried Jay about the right to dry, the New Yorker allowed that his countrymen "might give it up, rather than we [the British] should be dissatisfied about it, believing their People [the Americans] would not much value the privelege; and would in general chose to bring their Fish to their own Coasts as they used to do."[22] It is difficult to judge the impact of this disclaimer on Lord Shelburne, head of the British ministry, because it is not clear what his initial (pre-October) stance on the drying problem was. By September 18 he had decided to concede to France the exclusive right to fish and to dry along the entire west coast of Newfoundland—Vergennes had been pressing for even more extravagant concessions—and it may be that after September 18 nothing could have persuaded Shelburne to diminish any further the area of British dominion on Newfoundland. On the other hand, in August and September both Shelburne and George III seem to have been reluctantly contemplating the prospect of granting the United States some kind of privileges on Newfoundland.[23] It seems likely that Jay's cavalier attitude toward American drying rights reinforced their reluctance on this point and caused them to instruct Strachey on October 20 to forbid Americans to dry fish there.

Jay's draft of October 5 arrived in London on October 11. Some days earlier, however, the British ministry learned that Gibraltar, which had been under a close siege and for whose safety there had been fears, had been relieved, and this caused Shelburne to take a higher tone.[24] On October 17, the cabinet rejected Jay's draft and decided to send the pertinacious Strachey to Paris. In addition to giving him tougher instructions on the northeastern boundary and on American drying pretensions, it ordered him to negotiate vigorously for the payment of prewar debts and for the restoration or indemnification of the Tories.

John Adams

Strachey reached Paris on October 28 and engaged the American commissioners on October 30. By November 5 an express rider was carrying a new set of articles to London.

Adams was agreeably surprised by Franklin's performance in the negotiations. To his diary on October 27 he confided his fear that "Fs cunning will be to divide Us [Jay and himself]. To this End he will provoke, he will insinuate, he will intrigue, he will maneuvre." Throughout the negotiations, however, Franklin was the soul of compatibility, wringing from Adams the compliment, on November 30, that "he has met Us in most of our conferences and has gone on with Us, in entire Harmony and Unanimity, throughout, and has been able and usefull, both by his Sagacity and his Reputation."[25] The difficulties at the negotiations were not between Americans, but with the British.

Of the problems facing the negotiators two were resolved easily enough. When the question of British debts was raised, Adams declared that he had "no Notion of Cheating any Body," that legitimate debts should be paid. Jay agreed: he had, he told Oswald, "at all times jointly with his Colleagues declared that all that were Contracted before the War must be duely paid." Accordingly, on November 3, the American ministers stipulated that British creditors should "meet with no lawfull Inpediments, to recovering the full value, or Sterling Amount of such bona fide Debts as were contracted before the Year 1775."[26]

The northern and eastern boundaries between the United States and Britain were also settled without acrimony. In determining these boundaries, Adams took the lead. Strachey had brought with him one Roberts, a clerk in the recently abolished Board of Trade, who produced "a huge volume of . . . original records" in order to support the British claim to the whole province of Maine. Before embarking for Europe in the fall of 1779, Adams had had the foresight to secure from the clerk of the Massachusetts General Court an even more impressive sheaf of documents proving that the eastern boundary of Maine was the Saint Croix River. With these, he easily parried Strachey's efforts to put the boundary of Maine at the Penobscot River and fixed it instead at the Saint Croix. Strachey was more successful in getting the Americans to retract from the "Nipissing line" in the north. As alternatives, two lines, one along the forty-fifth parallel from the Connecticut River due west to the Mississippi and the other the river and lake line, which is the present boundary of the United States, were offered to him to submit to his superiors in London. The river and lake line was Adams's brainchild.[27]

The right to dry fish on Newfoundland, which Strachey was instructed to deny to the Americans, was hotly contested, with Adams leading the resistance to Strachey's efforts. "Since Mr. Adams came here," wrote Oswald on November 8, "the Commissioners have taken more notice of the Refusal of admitting their having the priveledge of Drying on Newfoundland than I expected from what they told me at settling the Plan of Treaty which was sent to England. But at last after a great deal of conversation . . . it was agreed to be left out upon Condition of their being allowed to dry upon any of the unsettled parts of the Coast of Nova Scotia."[28] The right to fish, as distinguished from the right to dry, was expanded from the October 5 preliminaries to include the Gulf of Saint Lawrence as well as the Banks of Newfoundland.

The Tories were the thorniest problem of all. The British cabinet had instructed Strachey to make a maximum effort to see that the United States either restored their confiscated property or compensated them for their losses. Failing this, the record must clearly show that the British negotiators had spared no pains to obtain satisfaction for them.[29] The American negotiators were unalterably opposed to compensating their "intestine enemies." The best that Oswald and Strachey could obtain was a provision which would allow the Tories to remain unmolested in the United States for six months after the evacuation of British forces for the purpose of settling their affairs and a meaningless American recommendation of "such amnesty and clemency to the said refugees as their respective circumstances and the dictates of humanity may render just and reasonable."[30]

Strachey carried the new peace terms back to London, where he arrived on November 10. After some days' deliberation, the cabinet sent him back to Paris to obtain adjustments in Britain's favor on the Tories and the fisheries. Negotiations resumed on November 25.[31] Despite instructions "to obtain as much satisfaction as possible" for the Tories, Strachey could not move the Americans beyond the trifling concessions and empty formulas to which they had previously consented. Rather than let negotiations break down over the Tories, the British ceased to press their claims.

Strachey had more luck on the fisheries. In view of Adams's later accounts of his fanatical stand for fishing rights at the peace negotiations, it is surprising that Strachey reported to his superiors on November 8 that the Americans did not appear to be "so positive" about the right to dry fish on the Nova Scotia coast, that they would give it up, "if objected to at home." Accordingly, the British cabinet instructed Strachey to deny the Americans drying rights on the Nova Scotia coast and, in a drastic effort to contract their fishing opportunities even more, to deny them access to the "onshore fisheries," those within three leagues of British shores. Adams made heroic efforts to have these prohibitions modified and at last succeeded in obtaining from the British not the right but the liberty for Americans to participate in the onshore fisheries and to dry on the Nova Scotia coast. Without these concessions he would have refused to sign the preliminaries, concessions that, nevertheless, by diluting right to liberty laid the groundwork for a century of controversy between New England fishermen and the British government.[32] The conflicts over the Tories and the fisheries having been adjusted agreeably to both sides, the preliminaries were signed on November 30, at Oswald's suite at the Grand Hotel Muscovite.

Four days later Adams wrote Robert Livingston, resigning all his "employments in Europe." He had consistently retracted his previous resignations of his revised peace commission, because he wanted to participate in the negotiations and because he did not want to gratify his enemies, whom he suspected of contriving the additions to the peace commission to disgust him and force him to resign. Now Adams persisted and mailed his resignation off to the secretary of foreign affairs, indicating, to others, that he would wait in Europe a decent interval for the arrival of official permission to vacate his posts.[33]

To leave Europe was the last thing Adams wanted to do. His resignation was a stratagem to force Congress to restore his commission as minister to Great Britain (for this is how he regarded his revoked commission to negotiate a commercial treaty with the British). "If ever a Citizen," he wrote Dumas on March 28, 1783, "could claim an office in equity, I have an incontestible Right to be Minister Plenipotentiary to the Court of Great Britain. Because I have had such a commission in my Portefeuille these four years." Adams expected no sinecure at the Court of St. James's. "I shall not be loved in London," he informed James Warren on April 9, 1783. "I have been as you know too old and odious an offender not to have Millions of Enemies there." But he would beard the British lion in his den not for his own good, of course, but for the good of the American people. "If Congress," he wrote his wife on February 26, 1783, "should think the Honor, Dignity and most important Interests of the United States concerned in an immediate Restoration of that Commission to me, I cannot in honor, and I ought not, from Regard to the Publick, to refuse it." His resignation was intended to force the issue. With peace at hand, Congress must appoint someone to Britain. Let it restore him to the position or recall him.[34]

Adams feared that Congress might exercise the latter option because of resentment (provoked, he supposed, by Luzerne) at the peace commissioners' ignoring the instruction of June 15, 1781, to put themselves under the control of France. "We poor Creatures are trembling here under a fearful looking for of Judgment and fiery indignation from Philadelphia," he wrote James Warren on April 9, 1783. Even if Congress did not take reprisals against him for his defiance of the French, Adams was afraid that, under French prodding, it might appoint someone else to London.[35] On the other hand, it might do the right thing and appoint him. His prospects were painfully uncertain.

Adams had other worries, too. The peace preliminaries appeared to be in trouble in the British Parliament in the winter of 1783 and their reception in Congress seemed to be far from promising. Repeatedly, in the spring of 1783, he expressed "anxiety" to correspondents about their fate in Philadelphia. In the period after the conclusion of the preliminaries, Adams was under great, if mainly self-imposed, strain. As he wrote his wife on February 18: "The Peace which sets the rest of the World at Ease increases, I think my Perplexities and Anxiety."[36]

Idleness compounded his discomfort. David Hartley, the minister designated by Britain to negotiate the definitive peace treaty, arrived in Paris toward the end of April 1783, but until then Adams had "nothing to do but think of my Situation." As he brooded about the revocation of his commercial commission, he grew angry. "Congress had been induced to disgrace me," he fumed. It had "stained and soiled me." "I would not bear this disgrace if I could help it," he went on. "I would wear no Livery with a Spot upon it. The Stain should be taken out or I would not wear the Coat." A "further disgrace," he complained, worse even than the revocation of the commission, was "waiting in Europe with the Air of a Candidate and an Expectant."[37]

More distressing than anxiety and anger was the ordeal of experiencing once again Franklin's phenomenal popularity in Paris, which had swollen to such proportions that Louis XVI ridiculed it by distributing chamber pots with the Doctor's face on the bottom. Adams had been in Paris hardly a week when he began to complain about Franklin's "omnipotence of reputation." So powerful was the torrent of adulation that no man, no accomplishment, could stand against it. What good was it to be "le

Washington de la Négotiation," the persiflage of the salon which Adams seriously believed was meant for him, when French pundits were predicting Franklin would "after a few Ages be considered as a God." The apotheosis of Franklin stoked up Adams's envy and animosity, which he handled in the customary way by projecting them upon the Doctor. "The Jealousy, Envy, and little Pranks of . . . Co Patriots" had been his worst obstacle at the peace negotiations, he wrote on December 4. His severest suffering in Europe, he wrote Livingston on May 25, 1783, had been caused by the "ill Disposition of the C. de Vergennes, aided by the Jealousy, Envy and selfish Servility of Dr. Franklin."[38]

As Adams mulled over the loss of his commercial commission, he reached the altogether predictable conclusion that it had been taken from him by the machinations of Vergennes and Franklin, who in this, as in all other instances, was driven by "envy and green-eyed jealousy."[39] (In fact, the commission was revoked at the initiative of James Madison; France's role was peripheral; Franklin's nonexistent.)[40] "Franklin's Motive was to get my Commission," Adams was convinced, "and Vergennes' Motive was to get it for him."[41] Adams had believed for a long time that Franklin and Vergennes were leagued together to persecute him, but the terms of their "alliance" had never been precisely clear to him. With information acquired during the preliminary peace negotiations, Adams concluded that he had discerned the full dimensions of the compact. It now appeared to him that with Vergennes, Franklin had concluded a bargain as corrupt as any in American history.

During the preliminary negotiations Adams learned that Franklin had concurred with Vergennes in advising Jay to negotiate with the British without obtaining, as a precondition, a specific acknowledgment of American independence. That Franklin agreed with Vergennes on this point did not surprise Adams, who had long criticized the Doctor for being too friendly, trusting, and even "obsequious" to the French. In fact, he consid-

ered Franklin to be a mere creature, a mouthpiece, of Vergennes. "Dr. Franklin is as good an index of that minister's sentiments as I know," Adams wrote Livingston on September 6,
1782. By Adams's calculations, then, Franklin should have
obeyed the congressional peace instruction of June 15, 1781,
which enjoined obedience to France. When the Doctor joined
Jay and him in flouting it—conduct in which Adams gloried on
his own account—he, Adams, abused Franklin for having
"meanly abandoned the System which he had pursued"—the
supposedly indiscriminately pro-French system. Adams also assumed that in deference to his pro-French system, Franklin had
favored, at the peace negotiations, Vergennes's efforts to deprive
the United States of the fisheries and the western lands. This
supposition contradicted the evidence of Adams's own senses;
Franklin had told him during the negotiations "that the Fisheries and Mississippi could not be given up." In fact, Franklin
had defended them so tenaciously that on November 29, in the
heat of battle, Adams exclaimed that the Doctor had behaved
"well and Nobly." The supposition also contradicted Jay's testimonial to Franklin on Sept. 11, 1783, of his steadfastness on behalf of the fisheries and the West. But Adams's suspicions of
Franklin had hardened to the point of not being amenable to
evidence, so that he persisted in believing that the "complai-
sant" Doctor had acquiesced in Vergennes's sinister objectives.
"Franklin he [Vergennes] knew would let him do as he pleased,
and assist him in inventing an Excuse for it," Adams wrote Warren on March 21, 1783.[42]

What was Vergennes's part of the bargain? Simply this—to
gratify Franklin's inordinate vanity, for which, Adams wrote
William Lee on March 15, "The feelings . . . of every American
Minister in Europe have been wantonly sacrificed." Gratification
was to be accomplished in two ways: by puffing up Franklin's
reputation—"He [Vergennes] and his Office of Interpreters have
filled all the Gazettes of Europe with the most Senseless Flattery
of him, and by means of the Police set every Spectacle, Society,

and every private Club and Circle to clapping him with such Applause, as they give to Opera Girls"—and by sacrificing his competitors on the altar of the Doctor's envy. Franklin, wrote Adams on April 13, "considered every American Minister, who has come to Europe, as his natural Enemy. He has been afraid that some one would serve his Country, acquire a Reputation, and begin to be thought of by Congress to replace him." Therefore, the Doctor enlisted Vergennes to traduce and destroy his colleagues. From this "detestable Source came the Insinuations and Prejudices against me, the shameless abandoned Attack upon me."[43]

The Franklin–Vergennes bargain was, then, as clear as it was corrupt. Vergennes would rid Franklin of his rivals and inflate his ego in return for the Doctor's acquiescence in his efforts to hamstring the United States. "It is," wrote Adams on November 8, 1782, "for the determinate purpose of carrying these points [depriving America of the fisheries and western lands] that one Man, who is Submission itself, is puffed up to the top of Jacob's ladder in the Clouds and every other man depressed to the bottom of it." Or, as Adams put it on May 2, 1783, Franklin "has aided Vergennes with all his Weight, and his great Reputation, in both Worlds, has supported this ignominious System and blasted every Man and every Effort to shake it off."[44]

The bargain with Vergennes appeared to Adams to be the perfection of Franklin's villainy. Enraged, he began pouring broadsides of abuse upon the Doctor. These fusillades have caught the attention of historians, who note that they do not "make very pleasant reading" and see them as signs of "psychological instability."[45] True enough, but the point is that Adams's outbursts in the spring and winter of 1783 do not represent an aberrant psychological episode; they are simply a continuation of the envy and fear that manifested themselves almost as soon as he arrived in Europe in 1778. Adams's tirades in 1783 differ from his earlier attitudes only in being more conspicuous. As he wrote Samuel Osgood on April 12, 1783, he had formerly been more reserved in his correspondence for fear that the British might capture it and use it as anti-American propaganda. "The Times however are past which required such Cautions." Everyone, he said, should write freely now.[46]

Adams took his own advice, for his attacks on Franklin were nothing if not free. The Doctor was a liar—"I can have no dependence on his Word. I never know when he speaks the Truth"; an imposter, the most egregious "since the Days of Mahomet"; an "unintelligble Politician"—"If I was in Congress, and this Gentleman and the Marble Mercury in the Garden of Versailles were in Nomination for an Embassy, I would not hesitate to give my vote for the Statue upon the Principle that it would do no harm"; "The Demon of Discord among our Ministers and the Curse and Scourge of our foreign affairs"—"There is nothing however black and infernal, that this Demon and his Imps are not capable of"; and, finally, a traitor—the conclusion flowed irresistibly from the conviction that Franklin would have tolerated the sacrifice of the West and the fisheries.[47]

Adams made no effort to disguise his views of Franklin and Vergennes. He wrote them back to America and aired his grievances against them in all companies in Paris. "I hear frequently of his Ravings against M de Vergennes and me," Franklin wrote Henry Laurens on March 20, 1783, "whom he suspects of Plots against him which have no Existence but in his troubled Imagination. I take no Notice and we are civil when we meet."[48] But the Doctor's equanimity at length deserted him and on July 22, 1783, he wrote Robert Livingston, risking, as he knew, a "Mortal Enmity," to caution him "respecting the Insinuations of this Gentleman against this Court, and the Instances he supposes of their ill will to us, which I take to be as imaginary as I know his Fancies to be, that Court de V. and Myself are continually plotting against him. . . . I am persuaded, however, that he means well for his Country, is always an honest Man, often a wise one, but sometimes, and in some things, absolutely out of his senses."[49] Adams's friends in Congress sent him copies of this letter, which confirmed his blackest suspicions about Franklin.[50]

Peace Negotiations

With the arrival of Hartley in Paris in April, negotiations for a definitive treaty began. By diverting Adams from his problems, the negotiations furnished a welcome respite from his anxiety and anger. This was true, even after it became apparent—as it soon did—that Hartley lacked the confidence of his superiors in London and would not be allowed to move the talks onto new ground. By mid-June the American ministers were convinced that the negotiations would, at best, only confirm the status quo. "We had by this time made up our minds," Adams wrote, "that the definitive treaty would be no more than a repetition of the preliminary articles of the provisional treaty."[51] And so it was. On September 3, 1783, Hartley and the Americans signed the definitive treaty that ended the long war between the colonies and the mother country and officially ushered the United States into the family of nations.

A recent writer has stated that Adams suffered another nervous breakdown a week after the signature of the definitive treaty.[52] He was, it is true, taken with a fever which incapacitated him for a month and which he compared to the illness that afflicted him at Amsterdam in the summer of 1781, but the evidence does not appear to support the inference that he suffered another breakdown. The Amsterdam breakdown was produced by a psychological trauma—the receipt of news of the alteration of his peace commission—but in September 1783 there were no traumas. On the contrary, there was good news. The anxieties that beset Adams earlier in the year about Congress's reception of the peace preliminaries dissipated in June with the arrival of the news that it had ratified the document. More importantly, on September 7 Adams learned that Congress had restored his honor by appointing him to head a commission with Jay and Franklin to negotiate a treaty of commerce with Great Britain. Adams was profuse in his thanksgiving: Congress, he wrote James Warren on September 10, "have tied me again to Europe by a new Commission so honourable to me, as to have really touched my heart"; the commission "does me infinite honour, and ought to silence forever every Complaint on my part for what is past." That a fever soon followed is indisputable, but it seems to have been no more than a recurrence of the fever that sickened Adams for a week in July. In fact, the "violent fever" that Adams suffered in September 1783 seems more likely to have been the influenza, which ravaged Paris in 1782 and was still abroad in the city in 1783.[53]

The conclusion of the definitive peace treaty ended an era in American history, changing the status of the thirteen colonies from a rebellious subject people to a sovereign nation. The peace did not, however, change the structure or intensity of Adams's jealousies or of his fears of conspiracy, which flowed along in their old channels. As far as he was concerned, the enormity of the corrupt bargain between Franklin and Vergennes had not been diminished in the least by the official termination of the war.

Franklin, Adams wrote Warren on September 10, "seems to have a positive Spight against every public service, that he does not exclusively perform himself. He opposes it and persecutes the Agent in it with a Malice and Rancour that is astonishing. I could have formed no Idea, that Jealousy, Envy and Vanity could have gone such lengths." And, of course, Adams still believed, as he wrote Samuel Osgood on June 30, 1784, that the Doctor was exercising his "low Cunning and mean Craft" to steal the position that was rightfully his, the ambassadorship to Great Britain. By 1784 Franklin was in a pitiable condition. Approaching eighty years of age, his health had deteriorated so badly that for long periods he could not get out of bed to walk around his room for exercise; when he departed Paris for America in 1785 he had to be carried to the seacoast on a litter. Adams was aware that Franklin had requested Congress to recall him, so that he might, as he told a friend, die in Philadelphia with his family. Convinced, however, that the Doctor "had secret hopes and expectations that he should be appointed to the Court of St. James," Adams regarded his resignation as a ruse. London was the old man's object and he would not, Adams believed, forsake his "clandestine Projects" to obtain the appointment there.[54]

Vergennes, of course, would assist Franklin by undermining his chief competitor, John Adams. Informed by correspondents in Congress that the United States in 1784 was considering imitating the Swiss in sending no ministers abroad, Adams was certain that the suggestion was the result of "sinister Intrigues" by the French to keep him from going to London. Let him be recalled, he wrote Osgood, and Congress would hear no more about the virtues of the Swiss system. Similarly, when Elbridge Gerry informed him in 1785 that his vanity had been attacked in Congress, Adams responded that the criticism had the "smell of French Politicks" to keep him from going to London. Let Congress be on guard, Adams warned Gerry, lest the charge of vanity cause it to exclude "the wisest, the most Virtuous and benevolent, the ablest and most disinterested the most indefatigble and successful Ministers that nature produces for their Choice."[55]

Adams was convinced that Vergennes's objective remained the same: to keep the United States dependent on France. If Congress allowed itself to be persuaded by the French to send no ministers abroad, it would have no means of composing its difficulties with other nations, with whom it would be "involved in eternal Disputes and Insults" and against whom it would be obliged to depend upon France for protection. Adams also believed he could see Vergennes's hand in the creation of the Society of the Cincinnati, whose formation had created disagreeable "Debates and Disputes" in the United States. The Cincinnati, Adams assumed, had been "concerted" in France with the purpose of weakening the United States—of overturning, perhaps, "the whole edifice of Republican Liberty"—so that a feeble and distracted nation would have to depend on French protection.[56]

The bargain between Franklin and Vergennes revealed itself to Adams most clearly in the Doctor's negotiation in 1783—at the king of Sweden's desire, it was said—of a commercial treaty that Adams thought procured fewer advantages to American commerce than it should have. Vergennes, Adams believed, had "all along discovered . . . a jealousy of American ships, seamen, carrying trade and naval power." Therefore, he apparently persuaded the Swedes to negotiate an illiberal treaty with Franklin as a step toward keeping the American marine weak, so that the United States might remain dependent on France. "This method of smuggling treaties into Franklin's hands alone," Adams wrote Gerry on September 10, "is contrived by Vergennes on purpose to throw Slights upon Jay and me, and to cheat you out of your carrying trade."[57]

The perfection of Vergennes's intrigues, in Adams's view, would be the appointment of Franklin to London and the Doctor's grandson, William Temple Franklin, to Versailles. Franklin, Adams recorded in his diary on January 11, 1783, had written a "Eulogium" to Congress on young Franklin, recommending him as extraordinarily well qualified to serve the United States abroad. "This Letter and other Circumstances convince me," Adams continued, "that the Plan is laid between the C de Vergennes and the Dr. to get Billy made Minister to this Court [Versailles] and not improbably the Dr. to London." What Vergennes would accomplish by this maneuver would be the installation of two of his creatures at London and Versailles who would give him a free hand in ordering American affairs as he pleased. Upon the United States he would impose "Ignorant Boys" and "dishonest Dotards in their second Childhood," who, under the color of cooperation with France, would betray their country.[58]

Adams responded to the continuation of these "plots and persecutions" by fleeing from them. In October 1783 he left France for an extended visit to Britain and then, at the beginning of 1784, without returning to Paris, he took up residence at the Hague. "I conclude," he wrote a friend from the Dutch capital on May 12, 1784, "to remain here without further Wandering and not to go to Paris at all."[59] Toward the end of July Adams received a letter from Thomas Jefferson, informing him that Congress had commissioned the two men to negotiate commercial treaties with the powers of Europe and that they were expected to do their business in Paris, to which Adams repaired in August with his wife, who had joined him after a separation of more than four years.

Adams, however, kept his eyes on the appointment to Britain. His hopes of receiving it alternated with his fears, for "having done enough to make three great Nations my Ennemies," as he wrote Jonathan Jackson on June 16, 1784, "it is not to be wondered at, that I have hosts who take fire at my name."[60] Finally, on February 24, 1785, Congress voted Adams the mission that had agitated him so long. He received word of his appointment at the end of April and went forthwith to Great Britain, where he was received on June 1 by George III as the first American minister to the mother country.

In London, Adams obtained some relief from the obsessive suspicion that Franklin was persecuting him. Britons regarded Franklin with profound resentment. He was "Dr. Doubleface," a Judas who had betrayed king and country to produce a rebellion. Absent, therefore, was the idolatrous adulation lavished on Franklin by Parisians, which eclipsed Adams's pretensions to fame and reputation and which prevailed in the French capital long after Franklin's departure in 1785. Had Adams remained in Paris he would have been envious of Franklin in absentia and would have handled his envy and hostility by projecting them in the form of persecution emanating from Franklin. In London it was not necessary for Adams to do this. He would have preferred, in fact, to forget about Franklin's malevolence altogether. "I wish it were possible," he wrote Arthur Lee on January 31, 1785, "to blot out the Page of History, and the Book of Remembrance . . . his [Franklin's] insolent Persecutions of you and me and others, and the Motives of them, a sordid Jealousy, and insidious selfishness, but it is not."[61]

Adams remained convinced of Franklin's "persecutions" of him for the remainder of his life. In 1800 he wrote of the Doc-

John Adams

tor's and Vergennes's conspiracy "to trip him up as Minister for Peace and get Dr. Franklin alone in his room"; in 1809 he denounced the Doctor's "irreconcilable hatred of me"; and in 1811 he complained of Franklin's efforts to "strike Mr. Adams out of existence as a public minister and get himself into his place." During his presidency Adams concluded that the Doctor's schemes were being revived by his newspaperman grandson, Benjamin Franklin Bache, "from whom he inherited a dirty, envious, jealous and revengefull Spight against me for no other cause under heaven than because I was too honest a Man to favour or connive at his selfish schemes of ambition and Avarice." More to the point, in Alexander Hamilton, Adams's principal enemy during his presidency, he believed himself confronted with someone very much like a reincarnation of Franklin. "Hamilton," Adams wrote his wife on January 9, 1797, "I know to be a proud spirited, conceited aspiring Mortal always pretending to Morality, with as debauched Morals as old Franklin who is his Model more than any one I know."[62]

It is remarkable, in fact, how much Adams's presidency resembled his diplomatic career in France and Holland, with Hamilton taking Franklin's place as his conspiring tormentor, whose consuming ambition was to supplant him. As president, Adams continually expressed his fears of Hamilton's "insidious and dark intrigues," of his "Intrigues and Cabals" to "turn him out" of office and establish himself as a "perpetual Dictator" in imitation of "Caesar, Zingis, Mahomet, Cromwell, [or] Napoleon." "Hamilton and a Party," Adams told Elbridge Gerry on March 26, 1799, "were endeavouring to get an Army on foot to give Hamilton the command of it and thus to proclaim a Regal Government, place Hamilton at the Head of it and prepare the way for a Province of Great Britain."[63] Hamilton was not, of course, an unabashed admirer of Adams, nor did he scruple to oppose his policies when he thought them wrong, but there is no evidence that he ever entertained the vast and diabolical designs that Adams ascribed to him.

Peace Negotiations

The persistence of Adams's hypersuspiciousness and of his tendency to see malevolent conspiracies working against him and his country may support those who suggest that he was afflicted, in some degree, with a paranoid disorder, the principal symptom of which is durable, inflexible delusions of persecution. But before such a conclusion can be endorsed, the persistence in large numbers of Adams's countrymen of the Revolutionary attitudes of jealousy and fear of conspiracy should be considered. Jealousy-suspicion was recommended to Americans in 1788 by both Federalists and anti-Federalists.[64] A decade later Thomas Jefferson extolled it—"free government is founded in jealousy, and not in confidence"—and during his presidency Andrew Jackson recommended "jealous anxiety" to his fellow citizens.[65] As for fears of conspiracy, the anti-Federalists, who are estimated to have been a majority of Americans, interpreted the movement for the constitution as a malign conspiracy, while both Federalists and Jeffersonian Republicans reviled each other as pernicious conspirators, scheming to destroy the public liberty.[66] Adams's suspicious, conspiratorial mentality may have been not a sign of pathology but simply a reflection of the climate of opinion in which he lived, which was, in the United States of the 1780s and 1790s, a product of the Revolutionary struggle with Britain between 1763 and 1776 in which jealousy and fear of conspiracy were pervasive. That Adams, during his diplomatic career and as president, indulged these attitudes to what often seemed an uncommon degree may reflect the uncommonly deep impression made upon a mind and a personality by a full fifteen years' involvement, from the Writs of Assistance episode in 1761 until the Declaration of Independence, in the heat of the Revolutionary conflict.

CHAPTER 7

JOHN ADAMS AND
REVOLUTIONARY DIPLOMACY

The turbulence of Adams's diplomatic service raises the question of how his ideas about American foreign policy withstood the periods of stress and turmoil which he experienced abroad. The answer is that his ideas survived his diplomatic missions with undiminished coherence. If anything, his commitment to them was strengthened by his diplomatic experiences, for the conviction which, in Europe, he found so unnerving and imperious, that a dynamic, malign conspiracy of the powerful was directed against him, confirmed the assumption which was central to his thinking and to that of his contemporaries, that power was aggressive and "propulsive"[1] and that it could, therefore, be best dealt with by being balanced and contained by countervailing power. For Adams, the theater of European diplomacy was, to reverse his admired Bolingbroke's famous aphorism, example teaching philosophy, for he believed that he had been the victim of power operating in its typically encroaching, insidious fashion and that, consequently, the value of the protective system of the balance of power was confirmed.

Bernard Bailyn has demonstrated that English Opposition ideology, which shaped the thinking of Adams and his colleagues, contained, as integrated components, both the conceptions of power as infinitely aggressive and of balanced power as its antidote. Other writers have recently shown that in eighteenth-century England these ideas were shared as well by the entrenched political establishment, the Court.[2] Domestically, the ideas manifested themselves in the commitment of all English parties to the classical ideal of "mixed and balanced" government. In foreign affairs they comprised what has been called the classical theory of the balance of power.

The situation in America was similar. The concept of the balance of power prevailed not only in Revolutionary thinking about foreign affairs but, as in England, it dominated domestic political speculation as well. Edward S. Corwin, the distinguished student of both American foreign policy and constitutional law, has argued that notions about balanced power which guided the Founding Fathers in conceiving the checks and balances of the Federal Constitution entered their thinking through the medium of foreign policy. "Thus was the Balance of Power," wrote Corwin, "borrowed from the stock teachings of the eighteenth-century diplomacy . . . projected into the midway field of federal government."[3] A case could be made that the reverse of Corwin's statement is true, that American ideas about foreign affairs were derivatives of domestic political theorizing. In fact, it is fruitless to try to establish priority for either the domestic or foreign arena as the source of American ideas about the balance of power. Balance of power thinking was pervasive in Revolutionary America, as pervasive as it was in eighteenth-century England, from whence it was derived.

This fact leads us back to the concern with which this study began: how peculiarly American, how revolutionary, was the diplomacy of the American Revolution, insofar as it was exemplified by John Adams. Questions about the extent to which the American Revolution was revolutionary are not usually asked by diplomatic historians. Colonial historians, however, are addicted to them. It is of primary importance to the colonial historian to know how much change the Revolution wrought. Historiographical schools have formed and fought over the question of the extent of revolutionary change, over contending claims that the Revolution was conservative or liberal-radical. Insulated from this controversy though they usually are, diplomatic historians are nevertheless parties to it, for they have come down hard on the liberal-radical side of it by picturing the Revolution as producing drastic change in the conception and conduct of American diplomacy. This view, to which most diplomatic historians subscribe, has been shaped principally by two writers: Francis Wharton and Felix Gilbert.

Wharton and Gilbert, and those who agree with them, may be said to be advocates of a "progressive" interpretation of American Revolutionary diplomacy. By "progressive" I mean that paradigm developed by historians in the 1920s and 1930s which held that American independence was achieved by a group of liberal, even radical, leaders who displaced a conservative colonial elite and who sponsored sweeping changes in American society. These liberal reformers are represented as being swept aside in the 1780s by a conservative resurgence that produced the Constitution and embodied itself in the Federalist party of the 1790s; the original goals and spirit of the Revolution are said to have been restored and vindicated by the election of Thomas Jefferson to the presidency in 1801. That Wharton and Gilbert wrote thirty years before and thirty years after the Progressive historians does not vitiate the applicability of the term progressive to their interpretation of early American diplomacy.

Both writers stress that the diplomacy of the new nation was controlled by bold, adventuresome men who produced profound changes in the way diplomacy had hitherto been conceived and practiced. According to Gilbert, Americans were "representatives of a new diplomacy," insisting on "proposals which were entirely alien to the spirit of the diplomatic practice of the time." "Traditional diplomacy and power politics seemed to be elements of a past epoch," "feeble structures which would fall at the first blowing of the trumpets of liberty." Wharton agreed. John Adams and his associates, he wrote, were "destructive rather than constructive, looking scornfully at all traditional systems of war, of diplomacy, of finance." Relations with foreign nations, they believed, "ought to be freed from the artificial shackles which international law had imposed" and be approached with "blunt simplicity," the expectation being that untutored freshness would carry all before it. Both Gilbert and Wharton see Revolutionary diplomatic radicalism yielding, after the first few heady years, to a more traditional, "realistic" style, in which transformation John Adams is represented as being in the forefront.[4] A season of radicalism, then a conservative reaction in the 1780s—this is their thesis. It is nothing less than a progressive interpretation of early American diplomacy.

Since this work rejects the progressive view of Revolutionary diplomacy, by stressing its continuity with earlier periods and by insisting on its old-fashioned European character, the reasons for its disagreement with Gilbert and Wharton should be stated. According to Gilbert, what was new, what was radical, about the diplomacy of the Revolution was the reverse side of its isolationism. The desire of American statesmen to avoid entanglement in the wars and politics of Europe and to confine their country's relationship with Europe to commerce, open to all nations, has long been considered isolationism and nothing more. But Gilbert contends that these aspirations were also "idealistic and internationalistic." His evidence is the alleged influence of the philosophes (French political philosophers) on the American Revolutionary generation. The foreign policy objects of the philosophes and the Americans—peace and free trade—were identical, Gilbert argues, and, therefore, he believes that Americans must have shared the philosophes' desire to bring about, through free trade, a "new age of peace" in which "relations between nations would become purely commercial contacts, and the need for a political diplomacy with alliances and balance of power would disappear from the international scene." Americans in 1776 must, in other words, have been idealistic and internationalistic as well as isolationistic.[5]

John Adams

I do not find that Gilbert presents any credible evidence that American Revolutionary diplomacy was "idealistic and internationalistic." That the philosophes, on whom he builds his case, shaped the Revolutionary mentality has never been conceded by historians of the Revolution (to most of whom, in fact, the possibility has never occurred). Gilbert offers no evidence from the 1770s to document their influence on American statesmen and produces only a few statements from the 1780s which even hint at a compatibility between their ideas and those of American leaders. Thus, his thesis would seem to be suspect on its face. Then there is Bailyn's recent authoritative investigation of the ideas behind the American Revolution which does not even mention the French philosophes.[6] Finally, there is contemporary testimony about the absence of the philosophes' influence in Revolutionary America. In his *Notes on Virginia*, written in 1781-1782, Thomas Jefferson conceded that French thinkers were virtually unknown in America; "We are but just becoming acquainted with her [France]," Jefferson wrote.[7] The smattering of information Adams had about the philosophes led him to scorn them. Their system, he wrote Benjamin Rush on December 22, 1806, "I took some pains, more than five and twenty years ago, to understand; but could not find one Gentleman among the Statesmen, Philosophers, and Men of Letters, who pretended to understand it. I procured the Books of Quanay [Quesnay] and I could not understand much of them, and much of what I understood I did not believe." The utter lack of influence of the philosophes on Adams is demonstrated by the reply he gave a friend in 1777 who was seeking to inform himself about political economy, about commerce and money in particular. Read Locke, Postlethwait, and Newton, Adams advised him.[8]

It seems possible that Gilbert assumed that the American Revolutionary leaders were under the influence of the philosophes because he mistook what the Americans meant by "free trade"—the panacea of the philosophes. This nostrum, as the

Revolutionary Diplomacy

philosophes concocted it, prescribed the complete elimination of tariffs, duties, exclusions, and monopolies; trade would be as free as air; each nation would specialize in the production of that which nature enabled it to do best and would exchange its products with its neighbors for the benefit of all. The network of salutary dependencies that developed would, it was predicted, guarantee the peace of all. Such a vision inspired few Americans in 1776, for the emancipation of commerce was not a goal of their Revolution. Quite the contrary. Americans willingly accepted the British mercantilist system under which they had prospered and were content to continue living within its confines. "We cheerfully consent to the operation of such acts [the Navigation Acts] of the British parliament," declared the First Continental Congress in October 1774, "as are bona fide, restrained to the regulation of our external commerce, for the purpose of securing the commercial advantages of the whole empire to the mother country." "It has been said," the Second Continental Congress advised the British people in July 1775, "that we refuse to submit to the Restrictions on our Commerce. From whence is this Inference drawn? Not from our Words, we have repeatedly declared the Contrary; and we again profess our Submission to the several Acts of Trade and Navigation passed before the Year 1763."[9] Finally, on June 8, 1776, John Dickinson reminded Congress that "we have repeatedly declared" that control over American commerce "was necessarily lodged" in Britain.[10] When John Adams drafted the Model Treaty in the summer of 1776, did he suddenly depart from these sentiments? Not at all, although a superficial reading of the Model Treaty might create the impression that it was a charter for free trade.[11]

The Model Treaty proposed commercial reciprocity rather than commercial freedom. It stated that, in its ports, the United States would treat subjects of a foreign power as it treated its own citizens, if the foreign power would do the same for American citizens in its ports. A foreigner trading to an American port would encounter no restraints at the customs house. American leaders, presiding over a predominantly agrarian nation, perceived it to be contrary to the country's interests to lay import duties which would raise prices to the farmer. But just because foreign merchants would pay no duties in the United States, Americans did not expect to be exempt from duties in foreign ports. The objective of the Model Treaty was not to immunize American traders against duties but to assure that foreign governments did not discriminate against them in favor of their own citizens. In insisting that Americans be treated as Britishers in British ports, the Model Treaty, in fact, accepted the Navigation Acts, for Americans would be bound by the whole system of "enumerated" quantities, prohibitory duties, and all the other appurtenances of mercantilism as they would be by the national mercantilistic system in French, Spanish, and other European ports. What the Model Treaty aimed for was the maintenance of the American carrying trade, by protecting it from the exclusions of the various national mercantilistic systems of the day. What was sought was participation in these systems, not freedom from their restraints.

The philosophes' infatuation with the reforming, redemptive character of commerce would have been incomprehensible to American leaders of 1776. Raised in a mercantilistic empire, they regarded commerce as a source of wealth and power. As such, they considered it a potential threat to their experiment in free government. Following Gordon Wood, recent writers have argued that the principal objective of the American Revolutionary leaders, which both domestic and foreign policies were designed to serve, was the establishment and preservation of a republic.[12] A republic was a concept of eighteenth-century political theorists who believed that there were exact conditions which assured its health: existence in a circumscribed area, absence of a standing military establishment, and preeminently the presence of virtue in the people at large. Virtue was understood in a civic sense, as a passion for the public good. Its antithesis, as well as the chief threat to republican government, was luxury, which was believed to breed corruption. Luxury was understood as conspicuous consumption to which one became so addicted that he fell into the power of, and was corrupted by, those who could supply the means to maintain the habit.

The principal purveyor of luxury in American society, the Revolutionary leaders believed, was foreign commerce, and they condemned it unsparingly. "Commerce produces money, money Luxury and all three are incompatible with Republicanism," wrote Adams, epitomizing American thinking on the matter. No less representative was Thomas Paine's statement in *Common Sense* that " 'Commerce diminishes the spirit both of patriotism and military defense' and would eventually destroy America's soul." Adams, in fact, declaimed almost nonstop against commerce. "The Spirit of Commerce," he wrote Mercy Warren on April 16, 1776, "Corrupts the morals of families as well as destroys their Happiness, it is much to be feared [it] is incompatible with the purity of Heart and Greatness of Soul which is necessary for a happy Republic." "We must guard," he wrote Mercy's husband, James, on December 15, 1782, against "that excessive Influx of Commerce Luxury and Inhabitants from abroad, which will soon embarrass Us." "The Intelligent advocate of Liberty," Adams informed Elbridge Gerry on April 25, 1785, is always against "the Commercial Spirit and innumerable other evil Spirits."[13]

It was not just Adams and men of his type who feared the corrosive effects of commerce. Merchants themselves were apprehensive about it. Tristram Dalton, for example, agreed with those who argued "against an extensive trade, as ruinous to the manners of a Republic." And Silas Deane, the tragic symbol of the Revolutionary merchant, shared the common sentiments about trade: "only by banishing wealth and luxury, and holding commerce the parent of both in abhorrence" would it be possible to preserve republican government.[14] Curiously enough, the very philosophes—Mably, Mirabeau, Raynal—whom Gilbert quotes as expecting free trade to produce a regenerate world order were warning Americans in the 1780s about the incompatibility of commerce and republican government. Mably was particularly shrill about the baleful effects of trade, stating, "I cannot avoid coinciding with the opinion of Plato, who, in order to secure the welfare of a republic, recommended that it should not establish itself either near the sea, nor upon the borders of any large river."[15]

What antidotes were available to the poison of unbridled commerce? One was proposed by Jefferson, who suggested that "it might be better for us to abandon the ocean altogether" and wished that "there were an ocean of fire between us and the old world." Adams expressed a similar view: "If every ship we have were burnt, and the keel of another never to be laid, we might still be the happiest people upon earth, and in fifty years the most powerful. The Luxuries we import from Europe, instead of promoting our prosperity, only enfeeble our race of men & retard the increase of population."[16]

But Adams and his colleagues knew that to abolish commerce was impossible. It was "theory only," said Jefferson, "and a theory which the servants of America are not at liberty to follow. Our people have a decided taste for navigation and commerce . . . and their servants are in duty bound to calculate all their measures on this datum." Or, as Adams put it, it was vain "to amuse ourselves with the thoughts of annihilating Commerce unless as Philosophical Speculations"; Americans were "as aquatic as the Tortoises and Sea Fowls" and "the love of Commerce with its conveniences and pleasures" was a habit in them "as unalterable as their Natures."[17] Therefore, the leaders of the new republic never seriously tried to limit commerce. But neither did they entertain any illusions about its being an instrument of regeneration and reform, much less of idealism and internationalism.

Felix Gilbert concentrated on the intellectual substance of early American diplomacy. Francis Wharton examined its form. Wharton believed that the radicalism of Revolutionary diplomacy consisted in its manners or, more precisely, in its lack of manners, for he portrayed Revolutionary diplomats as deliberately and enthusiastically flouting the conventions of European diplomacy. To their considered contempt of the rules of their craft he gave a name which is still current in the writing of diplomatic history—"militia diplomacy," borrowing the term from Adams who in 1782 wrote from Holland that "militia sometimes gain victories over regular troops even by departing from the rules." [18]

The most egregious transgression of the militia diplomats Wharton regarded as the vote by Congress, under their presumed influence, on December 30, 1776, of missions to a number of foreign powers—Austria, Prussia, and Tuscany—without its first ascertaining, as the conventions of diplomacy dictated, whether those countries were willing to receive American emissaries. What prompted Congress to dispatch this wave of ministers? Adams, who Wharton described as the "moving power" in Congress for the "multiplication of missions," [19] was not responsible, because he was in Massachusetts. Who, then, was responsible? The justification for Congress's action was that its duly accredited agent abroad, Silas Deane, urged it to send ministers to the various powers.

In a letter of October 1, 1776, which the Committee of Secret Correspondence acknowledged receiving on December 21 and which evidently produced the vote in favor of the multiple missions on December 30, Deane wrote, "It is of importance . . . to have someone deputed or empowered to treat with the King of Prussia. I am acquainted with his agent here, and have already through him received some queries and proposals respecting American commerce, to which I am preparing a reply. I have also an acquaintance with the agent of the Grand Duke of Tuscany, who proposes fixing a commerce between the United States and Leghorn, but has not yet given me his particular thoughts." In an earlier letter, that of August 18, Deane confided that Austria might also be favorably disposed to the American cause.[20] A passage in Adams's *Autobiography* suggests that someone else, possibly the Tuscan immigrant to Virginia, Philip Mazzei, a friend of Franklin, the Lees, and Jefferson, may also have been instrumental in producing the vote of December 30. Congress, wrote Adams, "had been advised, by Persons who knew no better, to send a Minister to the Emperor and to the Grand Duke of Tuscany because they were Brothers to the Queen of France. In this measure there was less Attention to the Political Interests and View of Princes than to Ties of Blood and Family Connections."[21] The point is that Congress voted the missions on December 30, on the advice of presumably well-informed persons who assured it that its emissaries would be welcome in the countries to which they were sent. Far from flouting the established rules of diplomacy, it honored them on this occasion.

It is also instructive to note what Congress did not do on December 30. It did not cover Europe with ministers, as men in the grip of "militia madness" would have done. No ambassadors were sent to what were called the northern powers: Russia, Sweden, Denmark-Norway. None were sent to Portugal, with which the colonies had carried on a lively prewar trade in fish and wine. And none were sent to Holland, with which Americans felt a strong affinity because of a similar religious and revolutionary heritage. Explained Adams to the States General in 1781: "It was not from a failure in respect that they [Congress] did not send a minister to your high mightinesses with the first whom they sent abroad; but instructed in the nature of the connexions between Great Britain and the republic, and in the system of peace and neutrality which she had so long pursued, they thought proper to respect both so far as not to seek to embroil her with her allies, to excite divisions in the nation, or lay embarrassments before it."[22] In July 1777 a proposal was made in Congress to send a minister to the Dutch, but the same respect for diplomatic protocol prevailed and Congress rejected the move: as Franklin wrote Dumas on April 10, 1778, because of a "desire to have and maintain a good Understanding with their High Mightinesses, and a free commerce with their Subjects, the measure was respectfully postponed for the present, till their [the Dutch] Sentiments on it, could be known, from an Apprehension that possibly their connections with England, might make the receiving an American Minister, as yet inconvenient, and if Holland should have the same good Will towards Us, a little embarrassing." Thus, the Congress in 1776 and in the years immediately thereafter consistently acted in conformity with diplomatic convention. Explaining its attitude, James Wilson wrote Robert Morris on January 14, 1777, "In our Transactions with European States, it is certainly of Importance neither to transgress, nor to fall short of those Maxims, by which they regulate their Conduct towards one another."[23] That American statesmen, flushed with enthusiasm over independence, engaged in, or approved, the nihilistic orgy of diplomatic rule-breaking which Wharton called militia diplomacy is false.

Adams, called by Wharton the "principal exponent" of militia diplomacy, was a model of diplomatic propriety. During his first mission to France he acquired and read a small library of books on the diplomatic history and practice of Europe. When he returned to America in the summer of 1779 he billed Congress for the books, since they were "calculated to qualify me for Conversation and for Business, especially the Science of Negotiation—accordingly the Books are a Collection on the public Right of Europe and the Letters and Memoirs of Ambassadors and public Ministers who had acquired the fairest Fame and had done the greatest Service to their Constituents in this Way." In other words, Adams wanted to learn how the experts had acted, so that he might imitate them. And during his first mission he acted every bit the professional. He refused to make an excursion into Holland because "there was no hope that Holland would then receive a Minister, and I thought Congress ought not to send one there as yet." Nor did he want to sally forth uninvited to other countries. To be sent to a court, Vienna for example, where he would not be received "would be the most painfull Situation imaginable," he wrote his wife on November 27, 1778.[24]

Upon returning to Europe in 1780, Adams continued to mind his diplomatic manners. Proceeding to France via Spain in January 1780, he passed within forty leagues of Madrid, but decided against visiting the Spanish capital because of "the political Situation that I might be in, my Country not yet being acknowledged as a Sovereign State, by any formal Act of that Court."[25] It was only after Adams became convinced that Franklin and Vergennes were conspiring to persecute him and to reduce his country to a demeaning and dangerous dependency on France that he threw away the diplomatic rule book and put on the extraordinary performance in Holland, which Wharton regarded as the essence of militia diplomacy and as characteristic of American Revolutionary diplomacy as a whole. Wharton, in other words, mistook an aberration in Adams's diplomatic conduct for the normal style of American Revolutionary diplomacy.

When Adams escaped from the orbit of Franklin and Vergennes and took his post at London in 1785, he renounced diplomatic iconoclasm and returned to his customary respect for diplomatic convention. In the face of Britain's refusal to respond to his inquiries and memorials about the frontier posts and a commercial treaty, Adams was the soul of tact. He specifically avoided demanding categorical answers, as he had done in the Netherlands. In fact, he was reluctant to put any pressure at all on the British. He had "not yet made a formal requisition [for the surrender of the posts]," he informed John Jay on October 16, 1785. "If I had done it I should have compromised my sovereign and should certainly have had no Answer." "It would be lessening the United States," he wrote Jay on December 6, 1785, "if I were to tease Ministers with Applications which would be answered only by neglect and silence."[26]

Observing Adams in Britain, Wharton concluded, as Gilbert had, that he had changed his approach and, profiting by his experience in Europe, had become a more traditional diplomatist.[27] But there is no evidence that, either in conceiving the strategy of American foreign policy or in setting its style, Adams swung from an initially "radical" posture to a conventional one. Except for the Dutch interlude, in which he adopted an unorthodox diplomatic style, Adams, in his thinking about foreign policy and in his execution of it, proceeded in a straight line from the Declaration of Independence onward, in a line that can be described as customary, European, and conservative. Insofar as he is representative of the theory and practice of American Revolutionary diplomacy, it reflects the same characteristics—characteristics that did not disappear until decades after the Revolution.

NOTES

Chapter 1

1. Felix Gilbert, *To the Farewell Address: Ideas of Early American Foreign Policy* (Princeton, N.J., 1961), pp. 89, 95–98.
2. Max Savelle, *The Origins of American Diplomacy: The International History of Anglo-America, 1492–1763* (New York, 1967), pp. 228–29.
3. Gilbert, *To the Farewell Address*, pp. 105–6.
4. Bernard Bailyn, *The Ideological Origins of the American Revolution* (Cambridge, Mass., 1967), p. 55.
5. Joseph E. Johnson, ed., "A Quaker Imperialist's View of the British Colonies in America: 1732," *Pennsylvania Magazine of History and Biography* 60 (April 1936): 113, 128, 130.
6. Richard W. Van Alstyne, *Genesis of American Nationalism* (Waltham, Mass., 1970), pp. 36–38.
7. Richard W. Van Alstyne, *Empire and Independence* (New York, 1965), p. 10.
8. Savelle, *Origins of American Diplomacy*, chapt. 20, esp. pp. 526, 549, 553.
9. Ibid., p. 553.
10. Adams to Mercy Otis Warren, July 20, 1807, Massachusetts Historical Society, *Collections*; 5th ser., 1878, 4:338–40; hereafter cited as MHS, *Collections*; Adams to Benjamin Rush, May 21, 1807, John A. Schutz and Douglass Adair, eds., *The Spur of Fame: Dialogues of John Adams and Benjamin Rush* (San Marino, Calif., 1966), pp. 87, 89.
11. John Adams, *The Adams Papers: The Papers of John Adams*, ed. Robert J. Taylor et al., 2 vols. to date (Cambridge, Mass., 1977–), 1:5; hereafter cited as *Papers of JA*.

12. Mayhew, *Two Discourses Delivered October 25, 1759* (Boston, 1759), pp. 60-61; Burnaby, *Travels through the Middle Settlements in North America in the Years 1759 and 1760* (New York, 1904), p. 149; Franklin to Lord Kames, April 11, 1767, Benjamin Franklin, *The Writings of Benjamin Franklin*, ed. Albert H. Smyth, 10 vols. (New York, 1905–1907), 5:21; Arthur Lee to Samuel Adams, Dec. 24, 1772, Louis W. Potts, "Arthur Lee: A Virtuous Revolutionary" (Ph.D. diss., Duke University, 1970), p. 148 n; Samuel Adams to Arthur Lee, April 4, 1774, Samuel Adams, *The Writings of Samuel Adams*, ed. Harry A. Cushing, 4 vols. (New York, 1904–1908), 3:101–2; Benjamin Rush to Arthur Lee, May 4, 1774, Richard H. Lee, *Life of Arthur Lee, LL.D.*, 2 vols. (Boston, 1829), 1:36–37; Edwin G. Burrows and Michael Wallace, "The American Revolution: The Ideology and Psychology of National Liberation," *Perspectives in American History* 6 (1972): 208, 209; James Warren to John Adams, Dec. 19, 1774, *Papers of JA*, 2:203–4; Hooper to James Iredell, Jan. 6, 1776, Paul H. Smith et al., eds., *Letters of Delegates to Congress 1774–1789*, 3 vols. to date (Washington, D.C., 1976–), 3:45.

13. Thomas Stone to James Hollyday, May 20, 1776, Smith, *Letters of Delegates to Congress*, 4:51; Lee to Landon Carter, April 1, 1776, ibid., 3:471, 2:248–49; Edwin G. Burrows and Michael Wallace, "The American Revolution: The Ideology and Psychology of National Liberation," *Perspectives in American History* 6 (1972): 221, 223.

14. Gage to Dartmouth, Oct. 1775, PRO, CO 5/763; Adams to Abigail Adams, Aug. 14, 1776, Lyman H. Butterfield et al., eds., *Adams Family Correspondence*, 4 vols. (Cambridge, Mass., 1963–1973), 2:96–97; to Edmund Jenings, Dec. 26, 1781, Adams Papers, microfilm ed., reel 355; Adams to Samuel Huntington, Sept. 25, 1780, Francis Wharton, ed., *The Revolutionary Diplomatic Correspondence of the United States*, 6 vols. (Washington, D.C., 1889), 4:67–69; hereafter cited as *Diplomatic Correspondence*; Samuel Johnson, "Taxation No Tyranny," *Boswell's Life of Johnson*, Oxford Standard ed. (London, 1953), p. 592; Adams to Hendrik Calkoen, Oct. 6, 1780, Charles F. Adams, ed., *The Works of John Adams*, 10 vols. (Boston, 1850–1856), 7:273; hereafter cited as *Works of JA*; Oct. 16, 1780, ibid., 7:285; Adams to

Horatio Gates, March 23, 1776, Smith, *Letters of Delegates to Congress*, 3:431; to Edmund Jenings, April 21, 1780; to John Jay, May 8, 1785, Adams Papers, microfilm ed., reels 96, 107.

15. John Adams, *Diary and Autobiography of John Adams*, ed. Lyman H. Butterfield et al., 4 vols. (Cambridge, Mass., 1961–1966), 4:38–39.

16. Jefferson to George Washington, March 15, 1784, Thomas Jefferson, *The Papers of Thomas Jefferson*, ed. Julian P. Boyd et al., 19 vols. to date (Princeton, N.J., 1950–), 7:26; [Arthur Lee], *A Speech intended to have been delivered in the House of Commons, in support of the Petition from the General Congress at Philadelphia* (London, 1775), p. 53; *Writings of Franklin*, 4:67–69; James H. Hutson, ed., *Letters from a Distinguished American: Twelve Essays by John Adams on American Foreign Policy* (Washington, D.C., 1978), pp. 41–46; *Writings of Franklin*, 3:71, 4:3; John Dickinson, *The Late Regulations Respecting the British Colonies* in *Pamphlets of the American Revolution*, ed. Bernard Bailyn (Cambridge, Mass., 1965), p. 687; Butterfield, *Diary and Autobiography*, 2:214; *Papers of Thomas Jefferson*, 1:219.

17. Quoted in Bernard Bailyn, *The Ordeal of Thomas Hutchinson* (Cambridge, Mass., 1974), pp. 234, 307.

18. Daniel Leonard, *Massachusettensis* (London, 1776), p. 61; Williamson is quoted by Van Alstyne, *Empire and Independence*, p. 73; [Charles Inglis], *The True Interest of America Impartially Stated* (Philadelphia, 1776), p. 64; Gerry to John Wendell, Nov. 11, 1776, Dreer Collection, Historical Society of Pennsylvania; Adams to Samuel Cooper, Feb. 4, 1777, *Writings of Samuel Adams*, 3:354.

19. Witherspoon, Speech to Congress, July 30, 1776, Smith, *Letters of Delegates to Congress*, 4:586.

20. *Works of JA*, 7:100; Adams to Patrick Henry, July 9, 1778, Adams Papers, microfilm ed., reel 93.

21. A Distinguished American (Adams), *Parker's General Advertiser* (London), Aug. 23, Oct. 17, 1782, in Hutson, *Letters from a Distinguished American*, pp. 4–5, 30; Adams to van der Capellen, Jan. 21, 1781; to Edme Genet, May 9, 1780, *Works of JA*, 7:161, 357; to Samuel Huntington, Sept. 25, 1780, Wharton, *Diplo-*

matic Correspondence, 4, 67–69; to Edmund Jenings, April 27, 1781, Adams Papers, microfilm ed., reel 354.

22. A Distinguished American (Adams), *Parker's General Advertiser* (London), Oct. 2, 1782, in Hutson, *Letters from a Distinguished American*, p. 27; Adams to Robert Livingston, June 23, 1783, Wharton, *Diplomatic Correspondence*, 6:500; to Edmund Jenings, July 18, 1780; to the President of Congress, Dec. 8, 1778, Adams Papers, microfilm ed., reels 352, 93; Edmund C. Burnett, ed., *Letters of Members of the Continental Congress*, 8 vols. (Washington, D.C., 1921–1936), 1:3; James H. Hutson, ed., *A Decent Respect to the Opinions of Mankind: Congressional State Papers, 1774–1776* (Washington, D.C., 1976), p. 108; Wendell to Franklin, Oct. 30, 1777, quoted in William Stinchcombe, *The American Revolution and the French Alliance* (Syracuse, N.Y., 1969), p. 11; see also Livingston to Thomas Lynch, Jan.-Feb. 1776; Robert Morris to Robert Herries, Feb. 15, 1776, Smith, *Letters of Delegates to Congress*, 3:179, 58.

23. Ian R. Christie and Benjamin W. Labaree, *Empire or Independence, 1760–1776* (New York, 1976), pp. 253, 254.

24. *Papers of JA*, 1:5.

25. *Papers of Thomas Jefferson*, 1:325; Adams to Samuel Huntington, June 17, 1780, Adams Papers, microfilm ed., reel 100.

26. *Warren-Adams Letters Being chiefly correspondence among John Adams, Samuel Adams, and James Warren*, ed. Worthington C. Ford, 2 vols. (Boston, 1917–1925), 1:314.

27. Adams to Warren, March 18, 1777, Adams Papers, microfilm ed., reel 91; Gilbert, *To the Farewell Address*, p. 17.

28. [Jacob Green], *Observations on the Reconciliation of Great Britain and the Colonies* (New York, 1776), p. 9. Green was not a Loyalist. The quotation here was one in a series of his statements of Loyalist positions, which he presented for the purpose of refuting.

29. [Charles Inglis], *True Interest*, pp. 57–58; [Thomas Chandler], *A Friendly Address to all Reasonable Americans* (New York, 1774), pp. 24–25; Joseph Galloway, *A Candid Examination of the Mutual Claims of Great Britain and the Colonies* (New York, 1775), p. 46; Leonard, *Massachusettensis*, p. 61.

30. Leonard, *Massachusettensis*, p. 61.

31. Galloway, *A Candid Examination*, p. 46; Chandler, *A Friendly Address*, pp. 24-25; Leonard, *Massachusettensis*, p. 62.

32. Dickinson, *Letters to the Inhabitants of the British Colonies*, in *The Political Writings of John Dickinson 1764-1774*, ed. Paul L. Ford (New York, 1970), p. 494; *Federalist*, no. 19, *The Federalist*, ed. Benjamin F. Wright (Cambridge, Mass., 1961), p. 180; Thomas Jefferson to John Adams, Jan. 11, 1816, *The Adams-Jefferson Letters*, ed. Lester J. Cappon, 2 vols. (Chapel Hill, N.C., 1959), 2:459; Butterfield, *Diary and Autobiography*, 1:36.

33. Chandler, *A Friendly Address*, p. 25; *Papers of JA*, 2:253.

34. Burnett, *Letters of Members of the Continental Congress*, 1:3; Hutson, *A Decent Respect*, p. 108; "The Farmer Refuted," Alexander Hamilton, *Papers of Alexander Hamilton*, ed. Harold C. Syrett, 26 vols. (New York, 1961-1979), 1:159-60.

35. Leonard, *Massachusettensis*, p. 61; Dickinson, Notes for a speech, June 8-10, 1776, Smith, *Letters of Delegates to Congress*, 4:167. Wrote Thomas Paine in *Common Sense*: "It is the interest of all Europe to have America a free port. Her trade will always be a protection." Thomas Wendel, ed., *Thomas Paine's Common Sense: The Call to Independence* (Woodbury, N.Y., 1975), p. 81.

36. *Papers of JA*, 2:179.

37. *Papers of Thomas Jefferson*, 1:217.

38. Butterfield, *Diary and Autobiography*, 3:315; Adams to Mercy Otis Warren, July 20, 1807, MHS, *Collections*, 4:349.

39. Smith, *Letters of Delegates to Congress*, 2:221.

40. Adams to Chase, July 9, 1776, Adams Papers, microfilm ed., reel 90; Chase to Adams, July 5, 1776, ibid., reel 346. See also Schutz and Adair, *The Spur of Fame*, pp. 38-39.

41. Butterfield, *Diary and Autobiography*, 3:328-29.

42. Wendel, *Thomas Paine's Common Sense*, p. 88; Inglis, *True Interest*, pp. 51-52, 66.

43. Cato, *Pennsylvania Gazette*, April 3, 1776. For Roubaud's intrigue and the fear in America of a partition treaty, see James H. Hutson, "The Partition Treaty and the Declaration of American Independence," *Journal of American History* 58 (March 1972): 887-96.

44. Smith, *Letters of Delegates to Congress*, 2:363.

45. Thomas Stone to James Hollyday, May 20, 1776, Smith, *Letters of Delegates to Congress*, 4:52.

46. Hutson, "Partition Treaty," p. 890.

47. Ibid., pp. 887-88, 893.

48. Ibid., p. 885.
49. Butterfield, *Diary and Autobiography*, 2:235; William Whipple to Joseph Whipple, July 29, 1776, Smith, *Letters of Delegates to Congress*, 4:566.
50. Hutson, "Partition Treaty," p. 890.
51. Ibid., p. 893.
52. *Papers of Thomas Jefferson*, 1:310, 313.
53. Cato, *Pennsylvania Gazette*, March 27, 1776; Inglis, *True Interest*, p. 64.
54. Richard Henry Lee to Landon Carter, June 2, 1776, Smith, *Letters of Delegates to Congress*, 4:117–18; Gerry to John Wendell, June 11, 1776, ibid., 4:188; Adams to Warren, April 16, 1776, *Warren-Adams Letters*, 1:227; Lee to Carter, June 2, 1776, Smith, *Letters of Delegates to Congress*, 4:118; Adams to Warren, April 16, 1776, *Warren-Adams Letters*, 1:228; to John Winthrop, June 23, 1776, *Works of JA*, 9:409.
55. Butterfield, *Diary and Autobiography*, 3:397.
56. See Smith, *Letters of Delegates to Congress*, 4:351–57.
57. Rutledge to Jay, June 8, 1776, ibid., 4:175; see also *Papers of Thomas Jefferson*, 1:310; Carter Braxton to Landon Carter, April 14, 1776, Smith, *Letters of Delegates to Congress*, 3:522.
58. Schutz and Adair, *The Spur of Fame*, p. 39.
59. William Williams to Jabez Huntington, Aug. 12, 1776; Edward Rutledge to Robert Livingston, Aug. 19, 1776, Smith, *Letters of Delegates to Congress*, 4:665; Burnett, *Letters of Members of the Continental Congress*, 2:54.
60. Josiah Bartlett to William Whipple, Aug. 27, 1776, *Letters of Members of the Continental Congress*, 2:62.
61. *Warren-Adams Letters*, 2:192.
62. Wendel, *Thomas Paine's Common Sense*, p. 123; Franklin to Howe, July 20, 1776, Smith, *Letters of Delegates to Congress*, 4:499; Paul L. Ford, ed., "Lord Howe's Commission to Pacify the Colonies," *Atlantic Monthly* 77 (June 1896): 758–62.
63. A Distinguished American (Adams), *Parker's General Advertiser* (London), Sept. 3, Oct. 2, 1782, in Hutson, *Letters from a Distinguished American*, p. 27; Adams to Samuel Huntington, June 16, 1780, Adams Papers, microfilm ed., reel 100; Adams to John Heath, July 10, 1778; to C. W. F. Dumas, May 19, 1781, ibid., reels 93, 102; Butterfield, *Diary and Autobiography*, 3:61, 68.

64. Adams to Samuel Chase, July 1, 1776; to Edmund Jenings, April 25, 1780; to Richard Henry Lee, Dec. 24, 1785, Adams Papers, microfilm ed., reels 89, 112, 351; to Jay, Aug. 13, 1782, *Works of JA*, 7:610; to Edmund Jenings, July 18, 1780, Adams Papers, microfilm ed., reel 352; to Robert Livingston, Feb. 5, 1783, Wharton, *Diplomatic Correspondence*, 6:243; Butterfield, *Diary and Autobiography*, 3:105, 115–16; Adams to Jenings, April 18, 1783, Adams Papers, microfilm ed., reel 108; Butterfield, *Diary and Autobiography*, 3:122; Rush to Adams, Aug. 14, Sept. 21, 1805, Schutz and Adair, *The Spur of Fame*, pp. 32, 36.

65. Butterfield, *Diary and Autobiography*, 4:237; A Distinguished American (Adams), *Parker's General Advertiser* (London), Oct. 23, 1782, in Hutson, *Letters from a Distinguished American*, p. 35.

66. Adams to Rush, Dec. 19, 1808, Alexander Biddle, ed., *Old Family Letters* (Philadelphia, 1892), p. 205; *Boston Patriot*, July 18, 1809; Jefferson to Monroe, July 11, 1790; to Jay, Aug. 23, 1785, *Papers of Thomas Jefferson*, 17:25, 8:427; Fifth Annual Address to Congress, Dec. 3, 1793; First Annual Address to Congress, Jan. 8, 1790, George Washington, *The Writings of George Washington*, ed. John C. Fitzpatrick, 39 vols. (Washington, D.C., 1931-1944), 33:166, 30:491; Plain Truth, Benjamin Franklin, *The Papers of Benjamin Franklin*, ed. Leonard W. Labaree et al., 21 vols. to date (New Haven, Conn., 1959-), 3:203; Jay to Robert Livingston, July 19, 1783, John Jay, *The Correspondence and Public Papers of John Jay*, ed. Henry P. Johnston, 4 vols. (New York, 1970), 3:55; Silas Deane, Diary, Oct. 3, 1774, Smith, *Letters of Delegates to Congress*, 1:139; Marshall, Speech at Virginia Ratifying Convention, 1788; Butterfield, *Diary and Autobiography*, 2:139; Lee to Patrick Henry, Feb. 14, 1785, Richard Henry Lee, *The Letters of Richard Henry Lee*, ed. James C. Ballagh, 2 vols. (New York, 1970), 2:333–34.

67. To Jay, Aug. 8, 1785, Adams Papers, microfilm ed., reel 111.

68. Gilbert, *To the Farewell Address*, p. 89.

Chapter 2

1. Adams to William Cushing, June 9, 1776, Adams Papers, microfilm ed., reel 89; for similar sentiments, see Adams to Benjamin

Hichborn, May 29, 1776, ibid.; to Mercy Otis Warren, April 16, 1776, *Warren-Adams Letters*, 1:223; Gerry to Adams, Sept. 29, 1779, Gerry-Knight Collection, Massachusetts Historical Society, Boston; Adams to William McCreary, Sept. 26, 1778, Adams Papers, microfilm ed., reel 93.

2. Bailyn, *Ideological Origins*, pp. ix, 95; *The Origins of American Politics* (Cambridge, Mass., 1968), p. 11; *Thomas Hutchinson*, p. 206.

3. *Works of JA*, 3:464.

4. For a discussion of the role of jealousy in America from the Revolution through the Jacksonian Era, see James H. Hutson, "The Origins of the 'Paranoid Style in American Politics': Public Jealousy from the Age of Walpole to the Age of Jackson," forthcoming.

5. John Dickinson, *Letters from a Farmer in Pennsylvania* (Dublin, 1768), p. 96.

6. Samuel Adams, "Candidus," Jan. 27, 1772, *Writings of Samuel Adams*, 2:323; Samuel Adams to Arthur Lee, Nov. 21, 1782, *Life of Arthur Lee*, 2:230; William Tudor, "Oration, delivered at Boston, March 5, 1779," in *Principles and Acts of the Revolution in America*, ed. Hezekiah Niles (New York, 1971), p. 37; Jackson T. Main, *Political Parties before the Constitution* (Chapel Hill, N.C., 1973), pp. 404-5; for the "republicanization" of jealousy, see Samuel Adams to Benjamin Austin, March 9, 1779, *Writings of Samuel Adams*, 4:135; [Tench Coxe], *An Examination of the Constitution of the United States of America*, in *Pamphlets on the Constitution of the United States*, ed. Paul L. Ford (New York, 1968), p. 151; *Federalist*, nos. 29, 38, 64, 70, *The Federalist*, pp. 228, 276, 424, 457.

7. *Papers of JA*, 1:136.

8. *Letter from Alexander Hamilton Concerning the Public Conduct and Character of John Adams, Esq.* (New York, 1800), p. 7; Mercy Otis Warren to John Adams, Aug. 1, 1807, MHS, *Collections*, 4:396; Sedgwick to Alexander Hamilton, Oct. 16, 1788, *Papers of Alexander Hamilton*, 5:226.

9. Paul Wentworth to William Eden, Dec. 22, 1777, B. F. Stevens, ed., *Facsimiles of Manuscripts in European Archives Relating to America 1773-1783*, 25 vols. (London, 1889–1895), 2, no. 234.

10. Lance Banning, "Republican Ideology and the Triumph of the Constitution, 1789 to 1793," *William and Mary Quarterly*, 3d ser., 31 (April 1974): 171.

11. James K. Martin, *Men in Rebellion: Higher Government Leaders and the Coming of the American Revolution* (New Brunswick, N.J., 1973), p. 34; J. G. A. Pocock, *The Machiavellian Moment* (Princeton, N.J., 1975), pp. 507-8; Gordon Wood, "Rhetoric and Reality in the American Revolution," *William and Mary Quarterly*, 3d ser., 23 (January 1966): 25. See also Wood, *The Creation of the American Republic, 1776-1787* (Chapel Hill, N.C., 1969), p. 17.

12. Rhys Isaac, "Dramatizing the Ideology of Revolution: Popular Mobilization in Virginia, 1774 to 1776," *William and Mary Quarterly*, 3d ser., 33 (July 1976): 360.

13. Schutz and Adair, *The Spur of Fame*, p. 61.

14. Peter Shaw, *The Character of John Adams* (Chapel Hill, N.C., 1976), pp. 64–66, 150–51, 186–91.

15. Butterfield, *Diary and Autobiography*, 1:lxiv; Page Smith, *John Adams*, 2 vols. (Garden City, N.Y., 1962), 1:71; Bernard Bailyn, "Butterfield's Adams: Notes for a Sketch," *William and Mary Quarterly*, 3d ser., 19 (April 1962): 252.

16. Bailyn, *Ideological Origins*, pp. 158, 380; *Thomas Hutchinson*, pp. 2, 15, 16.

17. Extract of a letter from Paris (in Paul Wentworth's hand), April 16, 1778, in Stevens, *Facsimiles of Manuscripts*, 22, no. 1914.

18. "I was born for Business; for both Activity and Study. I have little Appetite or Relish for any Thing else" (Diary entry, May 25, 1773), Butterfield, *Diary and Autobiography*, 2:82. Adams to Abigail Adams, July 26, Dec. 3, 1778, in *Adams Family Correspondence*, 3:67, 129. See also Butterfield, *Diary and Autobiography*, 4:77.

19. Adams Papers, microfilm ed., reel 93.

20. To James Lovell, Sept. 10, 1779, ibid.

21. Butterfield, *Diary and Autobiography*, 4:41.

22. Adams to John Trumbull, Nov. 5, 1775, Smith, *Letters of Delegates to Congress*, 2:304.

23. Adams to Vergennes, Feb. 11, 1779, Adams Papers, microfilm ed., reel 93.

24. Butterfield, *Diary and Autobiography*, 2:346–47.

25. "Silas Deane's Narrative, Read Before Congress," Dec. 21, 1778, *Collections of the New-York Historical Society for the Year 1888* (New York, 1889), pp. 154–55; Butterfield, *Diary and Autobiography*, 2:346–47.

26. [Arthur Lee], *An Appeal to the Justice and Interest of the People of Great Britain . . . by an Old Member of Parliament* (London, 1774), p. 62; Samuel Adams to Benjamin Austin, March 9, 1779, *Writings of Samuel Adams*, 4:135; "Deane's Narrative," pp. 175, 181; Beatrix Davenport, *A Diary of the French Revolution by Gouverneur Morris, 1752-1816*, 2 vols. (Boston, 1939), 1:461.

27. Jack M. Sosin, *Agents and Merchants: British Colonial Policy and the Origins of the American Revolution, 1763-1775* (Lincoln, Neb., 1965), p. 188.

28. Adams to Samuel Adams, Aug. 7, 1778, Adams Papers, microfilm ed., reel 93.

29. To R. H. Lee, Aug. 5, 1778; to Lovell, Sept. 10, 1779, ibid; Butterfield, *Diary and Autobiography*, 4:143–44.

30. Adams Papers, microfilm ed., reel 93.

31. In his autobiography (Butterfield, *Diary and Autobiography*, 4:145) Adams claimed that the offending letter was written by Hancock to Silas Deane. His description of it in a letter to Elbridge Gerry, Oct. 18, 1779, makes clear, however, that it was written by Barnabas Deane to Bancroft. Adams Papers, microfilm ed., reel 93.

32. To William McCreary, Sept. 17, 25, 1778; to Lovell, Sept. 26, 1778, Adams Papers, microfilm ed., reel 93.

33. To Lovell, Nov. 27, 1778; to Gerry, Dec. 5, 1778, ibid. The Deane letter is in the Franklin Papers, American Philosophical Society, Philadelphia.

34. To Abigail Adams, Jan. 18, 1779, *Adams Family Correspondence*, 3:149.

35. Ibid., 3:181–82; to Richard Henry Lee, Feb. 13, 1779, Adams Papers, microfilm ed., reel 93.

36. *Adams Family Correspondence*, 3:129.

37. *Warren-Adams Letters*, 2:75.

38. To Samuel Adams, Dec. 5, 1778, Adams Papers, microfilm ed., reel 93.

39. Butterfield, *Diary and Autobiography*, 2:345.
40. To Samuel Cooper, Feb. 28, 1779, Adams Papers, microfilm ed., reel 93.
41. *Adams Family Correspondence*, 3:175.
42. June 8, 1779, Adams Papers, microfilm ed., reel 93. A notation on this letter indicates that it was not sent.
43. To Lovell, Sept. 10, 1779, ibid.
44. To the President of Congress, Sept. 10, 1779, ibid. The passage quoted here was deleted from the letter.
45. The inclination of scholars to call Adams paranoid can be explained by the fact that delusions of persecution are the principal symptom of the paranoid condition.
46. Lovell to Adams, Oct. 24, 1778; Samuel Adams to Adams, Oct. 25, 1778; John Adams to Lovell, Sept. 10, 1779, Adams Papers, microfilm ed., reels 349, 350, 93.
47. John Wood, *The Suppressed History of the Administration of John Adams* (Philadelphia, 1846), pp. 225-26.
48. Quoted in Gerald Stourzh, *Benjamin Franklin and American Foreign Policy* (Chicago, 1954), p. 297 n.
49. Butterfield, *Diary and Autobiography*, 2:351–52.
50. Timothy Pickering, *A Review of the Correspondence between the Honorable John Adams . . . and the late William Cunningham, Esq.* (Salem, Mass., 1824), pp. 3–4. Luzerne to Vergennes, Oct. 8, 1779, Archives du Ministère des Affaires Etrangères, Correspondance politique, Etats-Unis, vol. 10 (Library of Congress transcripts); hereafter cited as CP-EU.
51. *Warren-Adams Letters*, 2:72.
52. Adams Papers, microfilm ed., reel 93.
53. To Lovell, Feb. 20, 1779; to Jenings, May 22, 1779; to Thomas McKean, Sept. 20, 1779, ibid.
54. Lyman H. Butterfield et al., eds., *The Book of Abigail and John: Selected Letters of the Adams Family, 1762–1784* (Cambridge, Mass., 1975), p. 214. In this passage the editors actually use the term jealousy, but they use it in the contemporary sense as a synonym for envy.
55. Butterfield, *Diary and Autobiography*, 1:25; May 3, 1756, entry.
56. Adams Papers, microfilm ed., reel 360.
57. Butterfield, *Diary and Autobiography*, 3:50, 85.

58. Adams to Lovell, Feb. 25, 1782, Adams Papers, microfilm ed., reel 104.

59. Adams to Mercy Warren, July 27, 1807, MHS, *Collections*, 4:357.

60. Adams to Warren, July 20, 1807, pp. 332–33, 346; Aug. 7, 1807, p. 423, ibid.

61. *Boston Patriot*, Jan. 18, 1812.

62. *Adams Family Correspondence*, 1:119; to Abigail Adams, Dec. 2, 1781, ibid., 4:250; to Mercy Warren, July 20, 1807, MHS, *Collections*, 4:335.

63. *Adams Family Correspondence*, 3:129; *Correspondence of the Late President Adams originally Published in the Boston Patriot* (Boston, 1809–1810), p. 74; Adams to Jenings, Adams Papers, microfilm ed., reels 93, 96.

64. For projection, see Henry P. Laughlin, *The Ego and Its Defenses* (New York, 1970), pp. 221, 226–27; Anna Freud, *The Ego and the Mechanisms of Defence* (London, 1968), pp. 43–44, 51–52, 122–23; Lawrence C. Kolb, *Noyes' Modern Clinical Psychiatry*, 7th ed. (Philadelphia, 1968), p. 404. For the central role of projection in paranoid disorders, see David Shapiro, *Neurotic Styles* (New York, 1965), p. 68; William C. Niederland, "Paranoia: Theory and Practice," *Psychiatry and Social Science Review* (Dec. 8, 1970), p. 4.

65. Luzerne to Vergennes, Oct. 8, 1779, CP-EU, vol. 10.

66. Butterfield, *Diary and Autobiography*, 2:358 n.

67. Adams to Mercy Otis Warren, July 28, 1807, MHS, *Collections*, 4:374; Luzerne to Vergennes, Oct. 8, 1779, CP-EU, vol. 10.

68. The expedition never materialized. See Samuel E. Morison, *John Paul Jones* (Boston, 1959), pp. 187–89, and Henri Doniol, *Histoire de la participation de la France a l'etablissement des Etats-Unis d'Amerique*, 5 vols. (Paris, 1884–1892), 4:230.

69. Butterfield, *Diary and Autobiography*, 2:369.

70. To Edmund Jenings, June 8, 1779, Adams Papers, microfilm ed., reel 93.

Chapter 3

1. Mercy Otis Warren to Adams, Aug. 1, 1807, MHS, *Collections*, 4:394–95.

2. Butterfield, *Diary and Autobiography*, 2:401 n.

3. To Mercy Warren, July 28, 1807, MHS, *Collections*, 4:372, 376-77.

4. Samuel F. Bemis, *The Diplomacy of the American Revolution* (New York, 1935), p. 79.

5. Burnett, *Letters of Members of the Continental Congress*, 4:69.

6. Cornelius Harnett to Richard Caswell, Aug. 31, 1779, transcript in the editorial files of Letters of Delegates to Congress, Library of Congress.

7. Henry Laurens, for example, thought Adams's appointment "extremely premature." To John Laurens, Sept. 27, 1779, South Carolina Historical Society, Columbia.

8. Gerry to Adams, Sept. 29, 1779, Gerry-Knight Collection, Massachusetts Historical Society; Adams to Gerry, Oct. 18, 1779, Adams Papers, microfilm ed., reel 93; to Mercy Otis Warren, July 30, 1807, MHS, *Collections*, 4:377.

9. To Lovell, March 4, 1780; to Lee, March 31, 1780; to Edmund Jennings, April 2, 1780, Adams Papers, microfilm ed., reels 96, 351.

10. Ibid., reel 93.

11. *Adams Family Correspondence*, 3:276, 281; Adams to Lovell, Adams Papers, microfilm ed., reel 96.

12. Worthington C. Ford, ed., *Journals of the Continental Congress, 1774-1789*, 34 vols. (Washington, D.C., 1904-1937), 17:466.

13. Butterfield, *Diary and Autobiography*, 2:346.

14. Luzerne to Vergennes, Aug. 6, 18, 1780, CP-EU, vol. 13.

15. Adams and Arthur Lee approved the disbursement. Adams and Arthur Lee to William Lee and Ralph Izard, Jan. 13, 1779, transcript in Papers of Benjamin Franklin Editorial Office, Yale University Library, New Haven, Conn. Jared Sparks unconscionably added Franklin's name to the signatures on this letter and Wharton followed him. Wharton, *Diplomatic Correspondence*, 3:22-23.

16. Memorial, May 1, 1779, Benjamin Franklin, *The Complete Works of Benjamin Franklin*, ed. John Bigelow, 10 vols. (New York, 1887-1888), 8:48-49.

17. To Arthur Lee, Oct. 10, 1778, *Works of JA*, 7:57; to James Lovell, Feb. 20, 1779, Adams Papers, microfilm ed., reel 93.

18. Butterfield, *Diary and Autobiography*, 4:65-66.

19. Adams Papers, microfilm ed., reel 96.

20. *Boston Patriot*, May 18, 1811, June 22, 1809.

21. To Samuel Huntington, Feb. 15, 1780, *Works of JA*, 7:121.

22. To Vergennes, Feb. 12, 1780, ibid., 3:260.

23. Franklin to William Carmichael, March 31, 1780; to John Jay, June 13, 1780, *Writings of Franklin*, 8:53, 92. Adams claimed, in a letter to Vergennes of Feb. 19, 1780 (*Works of JA*, 3:264), that he had "never communicated to any person since my arrival in Europe, the nature of my mission, excepting to your Excellency and Dr. Franklin, to whom it was indeed communicated by a resolution of Congress." This statement, contradicted by Franklin and by Adams's actions at his interview with Vergennes on February 11 and by his letter to the count on the following day, seems to have been made to extenuate his failure to tell Franklin of his mission; Adams could always claim that he did not think it necessary to confide in Franklin, because he assumed that Congress had already informed him of his mission's objectives.

24. *Works of JA*, 3:259.

25. To Mercy Otis Warren, July 30, 1807, MHS, *Collections*, 4:384.

26. To the President of Congress, Feb. 7, 1781, Adams Papers, microfilm ed., reel 101.

27. See especially Gérard to Vergennes, March 8, 1779, in John C. Meng, ed., *The Despatches and Instructions of Conrad Alexandre Gérard, 1778-1780* (Baltimore, Md., 1939), pp. 557-61, 563-66.

28. Doniol, *Histoire*, 4:4.

29. Gérard to Vergennes, Aug. 14, 1779, in Meng, *Despatches and Instructions*, pp. 846-50; Butterfield, *Diary and Autobiography*, 4:246 n.

30. Smith, *John Adams*, 1:460; see also Bemis, *Diplomacy*, p. 177.

31. Vergennes to Adams, Feb. 15, 1780, *Works of JA*, 3:261.

32. Francis Dana to Elbridge Gerry, Feb. 26, 1780, Franklin Papers, American Philosophical Society, Philadelphia.

33. Doniol, *Histoire*, 4:411 n.

34. Luzerne to Vergennes, Oct. 8, 1779, CP-EU, vol. 10; see also July 25, Aug. 6, 1780, ibid., vol. 13; Jan. 28, 1781, ibid., vol. 15.

35. To Samuel Huntington, March 30, 1780, *Works of JA*, 7:138; CP-EU, vol. 12; see also *Boston Patriot*, June 23, 1809, and Adams to Mercy Warren, July 30, 1807, MHS, *Collections*, 4:384; *London Daily Advertiser*, March 28, 1780. Meng, *Despatches and Instruc-*

tions, p. 120, is clearly wrong in his assumption that Gérard arrived in Paris "in the latter part of February."

36. Vergennes to Luzerne, June 3, 1780, CP-EU, vol. 12, demonstrates how Adams's stated desire to go to London confirmed this suspicion.

37. Luzerne to Vergennes, April 1, 1780, CP-EU, vol. 11.

38. To Samuel Huntington, May 31, 1780, *Writings of Franklin*, 8:74.

39. Vergennes to Luzerne, June 3, 1780, CP-EU, vol. 12.

40. For the date of Chaumont and Monthieu's visit, see Doniol, *Histoire*, 4:415-16; *Boston Patriot*, May 18, 1811; to Samuel Huntington, June 26, 1780, *Works of JA*, 7:207.

41. To Lovell, Sept. 10, 1779, *Adams Papers*, microfilm ed., reel 93.

42. Adams may have been right. Chaumont had been a party to numerous schemes in which Congress had been defrauded by currency manipulation. Thomas P. Abernathy, "Commercial Activities of Silas Deane in France," *American Historical Review* 39 (April 1934): 481.

43. Doniol, *Histoire*, 4:416 n.

44. Vergennes to Luzerne, Aug. 7, 1780, ibid., 4:417 n.

45. Ibid.

46. Richard B. Morris finds it "difficult to fathom" why Vergennes should have corresponded with Adams, rather than Franklin, about devaluation. The count opened the correspondence, of course, as a means of disposing of Adams. *The Peacemakers* (New York, 1965), p. 196.

47. Vergennes to Adams, June 21, 1780, *Works of JA*, 7:192.

48. That Adams had an interview with Vergennes on June 19 is inferred from his letter to Huntington of June 26 wherein he states that on his return from his interview with the count he "received a letter from Mr. Gerry informing me of the resolution to pay the loan office certificates." On June 24 Adams told Gerry that he had received his letter on June 19. See Adams to Huntington, June 26, 1780, *Works of JA*, 7:207, and Adams to Gerry, June 24, 1780, Adams Papers, microfilm ed., reel 96.

49. To Benjamin Rush, Sept. 19, 1779, Adams Papers, microfilm ed., reel 93.

50. Franklin to Samuel Huntington, Aug. 9, 1780, Bigelow, *The Works of Benjamin Franklin*, 8:281.

51. To Vergennes, June 22, 1780, *Works of JA*, 7:193.
52. Ibid., 7:193–202.
53. To Franklin, June 23, 1780, ibid., 7:203.
54. To Samuel Huntington, June 26, 1780, ibid., 7:207. Vergennes contradicted Adams's contention that he had sent Chaumont to see him on June 15. To Luzerne, Aug. 7, 1780, Doniol, *Histoire*, 4:417 n.
55. To Samuel Huntington, June 29, 1780, *Works of JA*, 7:208–10. Adams's friends in Congress did not mistake his message. On Oct. 12, 1780, the French chargé at Philadelphia, Marbois, reported that "he had been designated" in debates as Franklin's successor; on Dec. 15, 1780, Luzerne reported that the Massachusetts delegates "were exerting themselves in every way possible to induce their colleagues" to recall Franklin. CP-EU, vol. 14.
56. Vergennes to Adams, June 30, 1780, *Works of JA*, 7:212.
57. To Vergennes, July 10, 1780, Bigelow, *The Works of Benjamin Franklin*, 8:272–73.
58. Butterfield, *Diary and Autobiography*, 2:390; to Elbridge Gerry, Oct. 18, 1779, Adams Papers, microfilm ed., reel 93; to Abigail Adams, ibid., reel 350; to Robert Livingston, Sept. 6, 1782, *Works of JA*, 7:628; to Mercy Warren, July 28, 1807, MHS, *Collections*, 4:372.
59. *Boston Patriot*, May 18, 1811.
60. Adams to Samuel Huntington, July 23, 1780, *Works of JA*, 7:233–35; Vergennes to Montmorin, July 6, 1780, Doniol, *Histoire*, 4:424 n.
61. Doniol, *Histoire*, 4:419.
62. This was, in his view, a panacea that had, he informed Benjamin Rush on Sept. 19, 1779, been the "object of all [his] Negotiations" during his first mission. Adams Papers, microfilm ed., reel 93. See also Adams to Gerry, Sept. 11, 1779, ibid.
63. To Vergennes, July 13, 1780, *Works of JA*, 7:318–27.
64. Jonathan Dull, *The French Navy and American Independence* (Princeton, N.J., 1975), pp. 110–11, 155, 159, 164, 174, 179.
65. Vergennes to Adams, July 25, 1780, *Works of JA*, 7:235–40.
66. To Vergennes, July 26, 1780, Wharton, *Diplomatic Correspondence*, 4:7–11.
67. To Vergennes, July 27, 1780, *Works of JA*, 7:241–43.

68. Corwin, *French Policy and the American Alliance* (Hamden, Conn., 1962), p. 278.
69. Franklin to Huntington, *Writings of Franklin*, 8:128.
70. Vergennes to Adams, July 29, 1780, *Works of JA*, 7:241.
71. Doniol, *Histoire*, 4:417 n.
72. Butterfield, *Diary and Autobiography*, 2:446.
73. To Huntington, April 18, 1780, *Works of JA*, 7:150.
74. Morris, *The Peacemakers*, pp. 91-106.
75. To Huntington, April 18, 1780, *Works of JA*, 7:151.
76. To Huntington, July 6, 1780, Adams Papers, microfilm ed., reel 100.
77. To Vergennes, July 17, 1780, *Works of JA*, 7:229; to Vergennes, July 26, 1780, Wharton, *Diplomatic Correspondence*, 4:7.
78. Extracts from the Journal of Arthur Lee, in Lee, *Life of Arthur Lee*, 1:403.
79. Quoted in Bemis, *Diplomacy*, p. 18 n.
80. To Samuel Huntington, Aug. 9, 1780, *Writings of Franklin*, 8:127. For Franklin's diplomacy of gratitude, see Stourzh, *Benjamin Franklin*, pp. 148-61.
81. Butterfield, *Diary and Autobiography*, 2:446; *Adams Family Correspondence*, 4:35.
82. To Roger Sherman, Dec. 6, 1778, Adams Papers, microfilm ed., reel 93; Butterfield, *Diary and Autobiography*, 3:122; *Papers of Thomas Jefferson*, 1:325.
83. To Samuel Adams, Feb. 27, 1779, Adams Papers, microfilm ed., reel 93. Extracts from the Journal of Arthur Lee, Lee, *Life of Arthur Lee*, 1:404; to Vergennes, July 13, 1780, *Works of JA*, 7:224.
84. To Edme Genet, May 9, 1780, *Works of JA*, 7:161; to C. W. F. Dumas, Jan. 31, 1781, Adams Papers, microfilm ed., reel 102; Doniol, *Histoire*, 4:416 n; to William Duer, to James Wilson, Aug. 23, 1780, Deane Papers, New-York Historical Society, *Collections* (1889), 4:190-92, 198; to Mercy Otis Warren, Aug. 3, 1807, MHS, *Collections*, 4:410-11.
85. Franklin to Huntington, Aug. 9, 1780, *Writings of Franklin*, 8:128.
86. Adams to Livingston, Sept. 6, 1782, *Works of JA*, 7:628; Franklin to Arthur Lee, March 21, 1777; to Adams, Oct. 2, 1780, *Writings*

of Franklin, 7:35, 8:146; Franklin to Dana, April 7, 1781, Wharton, *Diplomatic Correspondence*, 4:354; *Boston Patriot*, May 18, 1811.

87. Adams Papers, microfilm ed., reel 93.
88. Lawrence C. Kolb, *Noyes' Modern Clinical Psychiatry*, 7th ed. (Philadelphia, 1968), p. 405.
89. To Arthur Lee, Oct. 10, 1782, Adams Papers, microfilm ed., reel 107; *Warren-Adams Letters*, 2:210.
90. To James Warren, Dec. 5, 1778, *Warren-Adams Letters*, 2:74; to Gerry, Sept. 10, 1779, Adams Papers, microfilm ed., reel 93; to James Warren, April 13, 1783, *Warren-Adams Letters*, 2:210.
91. To Mercy Warren, Aug. 3, 1807, MHS, *Collections*, 4:407.

Chapter 4

1. *Boston Patriot*, July 18, 30, 1809; *Works of JA*, 7:450 n; Benjamin Waterhouse to Levi Woodbury, Feb. 20, 1835, Woodbury Papers, Library of Congress, vol. 16. Bemis, *Diplomacy*, p. 126, confirms this observation, calling The Hague "a sort of listening post for European politics in general."
2. C. W. F. Dumas to Franklin, Feb. 5, 1781, Dumas Papers, American Philosophical Society, Philadelphia; John Quincy Adams, Diary, Adams Papers, microfilm ed., reel 6. Vauguyon did not report to Vergennes on Adams's visit.
3. Adams to Mercy Warren, July 30, 1807, MHS, *Collections*, 4:389.
4. Dumas to Adams, March 21, 1781; Lovell to Adams, Dec. 14, 1780, Adams Papers, microfilm ed., reel 354.
5. Justice to Dumas requires that it be noted that, in time, he won Adams's confidence.
6. To Robert Livingston, Feb. 21, 1782, *Works of JA*, 7:523.
7. Inferred from Adams's letter to Dumas, Jan. 25, 1781, ibid., p. 362.
8. To Mercy Warren, July 30, 1807, MHS, *Collections*, 4:387.
9. J. W. Schulte Nordholt, "The Impact of the American Revolution on the Dutch Republic," in *The Impact of the American Revolution Abroad* (Washington, D.C., 1976), p. 46.
10. James D. Page, *Psychopathology: The Science of Understanding Deviance* (Chicago, 1975), p. 293.

11. *Boston Patriot*, Sept. 16, 1809.
12. *Adams Family Correspondence*, 3:174.
13. Butterfield, *Diary and Autobiography*, 4:71–72 n; James H. Hutson, "Letters from a Distinguished American: The American Revolution in Foreign Newspapers," *Quarterly Journal of the Library of Congress* 34 (October 1977): 294–301.
14. "Boston," April 7, 1781, Adams Papers, microfilm ed., reel 354; *Boston Patriot*, Sept. 16, 1780.
15. To the President of Congress, Aug. 14, Sept. 19, 1780, *Works of JA*, 7:245, 249; to Arthur Lee, Dec. 6, 1780, Adams Papers, microfilm ed., reel 102.
16. Vauguyon to Vergennes, April 27, 30, May 5, 1781, Ministère des Affaires Etrangères, Correspondance politique, Hollande, vol. 544; hereafter cited as CP-H; to the President of Congress, Oct. 15, 1781, *Works of JA*, 7:472.
17. Isabel de Madariaga, *Britain, Russia, and the Armed Neutrality of 1780* (New Haven, Conn., 1962), esp. chapts. 6 and 7.
18. See Bemis, *Diplomacy*, pp. 157–59, for a good account of the Leede Neufville negotiations.
19. Quoted in Friedrich Edler, *The Dutch Republic and the American Revolution* (Baltimore, Md., 1911), pp. 157 ff.
20. *Warren-Adams Letters*, 2:154; to Gillon, Nov. 12, 1780, Adams Papers, microfilm ed., reel 102.
21. Madariaga, *Britain, Russia*, p. 271.
22. *Boston Patriot*, Sept. 12, 1809; to Robert Livingston, Feb. 21, 1782, *Works of JA*, 7:522, 534; to the President of Congress, Jan. 4, 14, 1781, Wharton, *Diplomatic Correspondence*, 4:227, 231.
23. Information from The Hague, Jan. 4, 1782, PRO, FO 37/4; *Works of JA*, 7:260 n, 376–77 n; Vergennes to Vauguyon, April 13, 1781, CP-H, vol. 544.
24. De Neufville to Franklin, Feb. 19, 1781, Franklin Papers, American Philosophical Society, Philadelphia; Adams to the President of Congress, Oct. 15, 1781, *Works of JA*, 7:472–73, 366 n; Intelligence to Sir Joseph Yorke, Feb. 22, 1781, PRO, FO 37/1.
25. To Dumas, Jan. 25, 1781, *Works of JA*, 7:361; to Philip Mazzei, July 3, 1782; to Edmund Jenings, July 9, 1782; to John Jay, Aug. 10, 1782; Adams Papers, microfilm ed., reels 107, 357; to Robert Livingston, Sept. 17, 1782, *Works of JA*, 7:637–38.
26. To de Neufville, Feb. 19, 1781, Adams Papers, microfilm ed., reel

354; to Bicker, Feb. 20, 1781; to Dumas, Feb. 2, 1781, *Works of JA*, 7:370, 364; to Adams, Feb. 5, 1781; to Jenings, Jan. 3, 1781, Adams Papers, microfilm ed., reel 354.

27. Vergennes to Luzerne, March 5 [misdated Feb. 5], 1780, Jan. 9, Feb. 19, 1781, CP-EU, vols. 11, 15.

28. Bemis, *Diplomacy,* p. 145.

29. Vergennes to Vauguyon, Dec. 7, 1781, CP-H, vol. 546; "X" to Yorke, April 29, 1782, PRO, FO 37/4; Thulemeyer to Frederick, Aug. 9, 1782, in H. T. Colenbrander, ed., "Depeches van Thulemeyer, 1763–1788," *Historisch Genootschop*, 3d ser., 30 (1912): 325–29; see also Vauguyon to Vergennes, Aug. 9, 1782, CP-H, vol. 550.

30. See, for example, Vergennes to Vauguyon, Jan. 18, 28, Sept. 27, 1781, CP-H, vols. 543, 546; Vauguyon to Vergennes, Jan. 9, 12, June 26, 1781, March 15, 1782, CP-H, vols. 543, 544, 547.

31. *Boston Patriot*, Sept. 12, 1809.

32. Vergennes to Vauguyon, Aug. 9, 1781, CP-H, vol. 545; Adams to Dana, March 12, 1781, *Works of JA*, 7:378.

33. Adams to Livingston, *Works of JA*, 7:522; Waterhouse to Levi Woodbury, Feb. 20, 1835, Woodbury Papers, vol. 16, Library of Congress.

34. Vergennes to Vauguyon, CP-H, vol. 543.

35. Thulemeyer to Frederick, April 20, 1781, "Depeches van Thulemeyer," p. 252; Vauguyon to Vergennes, March 13, May 11, 15, 1781; Vergennes to Vauguyon, May 11, 1781, CP-H, vols, 543, 544.

36. *Journals of the Continental Congress*, 18:1147; *Boston Patriot*, Oct. 6, 1809; Adams to Dana, Feb. 8, 1781, *Works of JA*, 7:368; *Journals of the Continental Congress*, 19:42.

37. Dumas to Adams, Feb. 9, 10, 1781, Adams Papers, microfilm ed., reel 354; Adams to Robert Livingston, Feb. 19, 1782, *Works of JA*, 7:517.

38. "Her [Spain's] determinations appear to be solely the fruit of the negotiations of the Court of Versailles," wrote Adams to Congress on Aug. 4, 1779, *Works of JA*, 7:105. In fact, Spain's prickly diplomatic independence of France at times drove Vergennes virtually to despair. Samuel F. Bemis's *Hussey-Cumberland Mission and American Independence* (Princeton, N.J., 1931) exhaustively illustrates this point.

39. *Boston Patriot*, Oct. 6, 1809.
40. *Works of JA*, 7:373–75.
41. To Dana, March 12, 1781, ibid., 7:378.
42. Dumas to Adams, March 10, 1781, ibid., 7:375; March 21, 30, April 2, 18, 1781, Adams Papers, microfilm ed., reel 354.
43. *Works of JA*, 7:378.
44. Adams to Franklin, Feb. 20, 1782, ibid., 7:519; Vergennes to Verac, Jan. 30, 1781, quoted in Madariaga, *Britain, Russia*, pp. 276–77; Vergennes to Vauguyon, Jan. 28, 1781, CP-H, vol. 543.
45. Vauguyon to Vergennes, March 13, 1781, CP-H, vol. 543.
46. *Boston Patriot*, 1810.
47. To Mercy Warren, July 30, 1807, MHS, *Collections*, 4:388; to Livingston, Feb. 21, 1782, *Works of JA*, 7:523.
48. Herbert E. Klingelhofer, ed., "Matthew Ridley's Diary during the Peace Negotiations of 1782," *William and Mary Quarterly*, 3d ser., 20 (January 1963): 99-100; Franklin to Adams, May 11, 1781, in which Franklin acknowledges receipt of Adams's letter of April 27, notifying him that he had received a ministerial commission to the Netherlands. The point is that Adams felt "menaced" by Franklin well before May 1781. Adams Papers, microfilm ed., reel 354.
49. Benjamin Waterhouse to Levi Woodbury, Feb. 20, 1835, Woodbury Papers, vol. 16.
50. Dumas to Adams, April 14, 1781, Adams Papers, microfilm ed., reel 354; Adams to Vauguyon, April 16, 1781; Vauguyon to Adams, April 17, 1781, *Works of JA*, 7:388–90.
51. *Works of JA*, 7:405 n. For a somewhat different account of the interview, see Adams to Livingston, Feb. 21, 1782, ibid., 7:528.
52. Ibid., p. 405 n.
53. To Lovell, Feb. 25, 1782, Adams Papers, microfilm ed., reel 104; to Livingston, Feb. 19, 21, 1782, *Works of JA*, 7:516, 524; Vauguyon to Vergennes, April 21, 1781, CP-H, vol. 544.
54. *Works of JA*, 7:405-6 n.
55. Vauguyon to Vergennes, April 21, 1781, CP-H, vol. 544; Adams to Livingston, Feb. 19, 1782, *Works of JA*, 7:515; Waterhouse to Levi Woodbury, Feb. 20, 1835, Woodbury Papers, vol. 16.
56. Lyman H. Butterfield, "John Adams and the Beginnings of Netherlands-American Friendship, 1780–1788," in *Butterfield in Holland* (Cambridge, Mass., 1961), p. 50.

57. To Robert Livingston, Feb. 21, 1782, *Works of JA*, 7:528, 521–30.

58. Stinchcombe, *The American Revolution*, pp. 140–41.

59. *Works of JA*, 7:365–66 n. See also Adams to Livingston, Feb. 21, 1782, ibid., 7:529; to Tristram Dalton, March 5, 1785, Adams Papers, microfilm ed., reel 107. "As to the consequences it could have, everyone maintains a profound silence" (Dumas to Adams, May 18, 1781, ibid., reel 354). Dumas to Livingston, Feb. 21, 1782, *Works of JA*, 7:525. See also Adams to William Gordon, April 15, 1783, Adams Papers, microfilm ed., reel 108.

60. Madariaga, *Britain, Russia*, pp. 309, 311–12; Vauguyon to Vergennes, April 24, 1781, CP-H, vol. 544.

61. See, for example, Stormont to Wentworth, Jan. 14, 1782, PRO, FO 37/3.

62. Adams to Livingston, Feb. 21, 1782, *Works of JA*, 7:529.

63. CP-H, vol. 544; see also Vauguyon to Vergennes, May 15, 1781, ibid.

64. May 11, 21, 1781, PRO, FO 37/1.

65. Vauguyon to Vergennes, March 27, 1781, CP-H, vol. 543.

66. Report, May 21, 1781, PRO, FO 37/1.

67. Vauguyon to Vergennes, July 3, 6, 13, Aug. 3, 7, 17, 21, Dec. 6, 1781; Vergennes to Vauguyon, Aug. 9, 1781, CP-H, vols. 545, 546; Adams to Livingston, Sept. 4, 1782, *Works of JA*, 7:621.

68. To Livingston, Feb. 21, 1782, *Works of JA*, 7:529.

69. CP-H, vol. 544; Bemis, *Diplomacy*, p. 93.

70. Vergennes to Joly de Fleury, Aug. 23, 1781; Vauguyon note, Aug. 28, 1781; Vauguyon to Vergennes, Dec. 4, 1781, CP-H, vols. 545, 546. Failure of the original plan, however, was caused by political considerations rather more than by the fiasco of Adams's memorial.

71. Vergennes to Berenger, May 31, 1781, ibid., vol. 544; Adams to Berenger, June 8, 1781, *Works of JA*, 7:426.

72. Morris, *The Peacemakers*, p. 207.

73. *Works of JA*, 7:434, 438, 443, 446–47.

74. Ibid., p. 450 n.

75. Morris, *The Peacemakers*, p. 210.

76. Bemis, *Diplomacy*, p. 187; Madariaga, *Britain, Russia*, p. 328.

77. *Writings of Franklin*, 8:291; *Works of JA*, 7:480; Franklin to Adams, Aug. 16, 1781, ibid., 7:456; *Journals of the Continental Congress*, 20:638–48.

78. Shaw, *The Character of John Adams*, pp. 150–51.
79. To Abigail Adams, Oct. 9, 1781, *Adams Family Correspondence*, 4:224; to Franklin, Oct. 4, 1781, *Works of JA*, 7:465; to Thomas McKean, Oct. 15, 1781; to James Searle, Oct. 20, 1781, Adams Papers, microfilm ed., reels 104, 102; to Abigail Adams, Oct. 9, 1781, Aug. 17, 1782, *Adams Family Correspondence*, 4:224, 364.
80. Doniol, *Histoire*, 4:417 n, 552, 583–84, 590.
81. For a recent account of Luzerne's manipulation of Congress to produce the commission and instructions of 1781, see Stinchcombe, *The American Revolution*, pp. 153–69.
82. Burnett, *Letters of Members of the Continental Congress*, 6:125.
83. Wharton, *Diplomatic Correspondence*, 4:18–19.
84. Franklin to Samuel Huntington, Aug. 9, 1780; Franklin to Adams, Oct. 8, 1780, *Writings of Franklin*, 8:126–28, 148.
85. *Adams Family Correspondence*, 4:175, 179, 190–91.
86. Adams to Jenings, July 20, 1782, Adams Papers, microfilm ed., reel 357; to Mercy Otis Warren, Aug. 3, 1807, MHS, *Collections*, 4:414.
87. Adams to Franklin, Oct. 4, 1781, redated Oct. 26, 1781, Adams Papers, microfilm ed., reel 104; to President of Congress, Oct. 15, 1781, *Works of JA*, 7:475.
88. *Boston Patriot*, June 12, 1811.

Chapter 5

1. Vauguyon to Vergennes, Feb. 12, 1782, Nov. 27, Dec. 15, 1781, Feb. 18, 1782, CP-H, vols. 546, 547.
2. Vergennes to Vauguyon, Nov. 29, Dec. 7, 1781, ibid., vol. 546.
3. Morris, *The Peacemakers*, pp. 254–56, 261; Madariaga, *Britain, Russia*, pp. 387–91.
4. Vauguyon to Vergennes, Feb. 18, 1782, CP-H, vol. 547; Paul Wentworth, note, Feb. [11–14?], 1782, PRO, FO 37/3.
5. Vauguyon to Vergennes, Feb. 12, 26, 1782, CP-H, vol. 547; Wentworth to Stormont, Feb. 16, March 7, 15, 1782, PRO, FO 37/3.
6. Adams to Livingston, Feb. 19, 1782, *Works of JA*, 7:514; Vauguyon to Vergennes, Feb. 12, 1782, CP-H, vol. 547.
7. Vauguyon to Vergennes, March 5, 20, 1782, CP-H, vol. 547.

8. Vauguyon to Vergennes, Dec. 15, 1781, ibid., vol. 546.

9. To the President of Congress, Dec. 18, 1781, Jan, 14, 1782, *Works of JA*, 7:497–98, 504–8; *Boston Patriot*, Sept. 19, 1810.

10. Stormont to Wentworth, Jan. 14, 1782; Wentworth to Stormont, Feb. 1, 11, March 31, 1782, PRO, FO 37/3; Vauguyon to Vergennes, Feb. 12, 1782, CP-H, vol. 547.

11. Vauguyon to Vergennes, Jan. 23, 26, Feb. 20, April 6, 1781; Vergennes to Vauguyon, Feb. 8, Dec. 7, 1781, CP-H, vols. 543, 544, 546; Wentworth to Stormont, Feb. 11, 1782, PRO, FO 37/3; Adams to Livingston, Feb. 21, 1782, *Works of JA*, 7:529; Vauguyon to Vergennes, Feb. 18, 1782, CP-H, vol. 547; Wentworth to Stormont, March 15, 1782, PRO, FO 37/3.

12. Wentworth to Stormont, Feb. 11, 16, 23, March 7, 12, 31, 1782, PRO, FO 37/3.

13. Vauguyon to Vergennes, Feb. 18, 1782, CP-H, vol. 547; Stormont to Wentworth, Jan. 14, March 8, 1782, PRO, FO 37/3; Vauguyon to Vergennes, Dec. 6, 1781, CP-H, vol. 546.

14. Vauguyon to Vergennes, Dec. 6, 1781, CP-H, vol. 546; Wentworth to Stormont, Feb. 23, 1782, PRO, FO 37/3; Adams to Dana, March 15, 1782, *Works of JA*, 7:543.

15. British informant, The Hague, March 1, 1782, PRO, FO 37/3.

16. Vauguyon to Vergennes, March 19, 20, 22, 1782, CP-H, vol. 547.

17. Wentworth to Stormont, March 31, 1782, PRO, FO 37/3; Vauguyon to Vergennes, March 22, 1782, CP-H, vol. 547.

18. Vauguyon to Vergennes, March 29, 1782, CP-H, vol. 547.

19. British informant, The Hague, March 5, 1782, PRO, FO 37/3.

20. Ibid., April 23, 1782, PRO, FO 37/4.

21. To Edmund Jenings, Adams Papers, microfilm ed., reel 102; to Robert Livingston, Feb. 14, 1782; to Dana, March 15, 1782, *Works of JA*, 7:511, 543.

22. To van der Capellen, Jan. 14, 1782, *Works of JA*, 7:503.

23. Adams to Robert Livingston, March 11, 1782; Dumas to Adams, March 16, 1782, ibid., 7:538, 547; *Boston Patriot*, Jan. 5, 1811; Adams to Mercy Warren, July 30, 1807, MHS, *Collections*, 4:387.

24. Vergennes to Vauguyon, Sept. 27, 1781, March 13, 1782; Vauguyon to Vergennes, Feb. 26, March 15, 20, 26, 1782; Vergennes to Vauguyon, March 7, 13, 1782, CP-H, vols. 546, 547.

25. *Works of JA*, 7:555.

26. To Gordon, Adams Papers, microfilm ed., reel 108.

27. *Boston Patriot*, Jan. 5, 1811.

28. Vergennes to Luzerne, Feb. 19, 1781, CP-EU, vol. 15.

29. Vergennes to Vauguyon, April 27, 1782, CP-H, vol. 547.

30. To Abigail Adams, July 1, Aug. 15, 1782, *Adams Family Correspondence*, 4:338, 361.

31. *Boston Patriot*, July 27, 1809; to Bondfield, Jan. 3, 1783; to William Lee, March 15, 1783; to Elbridge Gerry, Sept. 8, 1783, Adams Papers, microfilm ed., reel 108; to James Warren, Dec. 15, 1782, *Warren-Adams Letters*, 2:187.

32. Morris, *The Peacemakers*, p. 253.

33. Vauguyon to Vergennes, CP-H, vol. 547; Wentworth to Stormont, March 7, 1782; Rendorp to Wentworth, March 22, 1782, PRO, FO 37/3.

34. Adams to Robert Livingston, April 23, Sept. 17, Oct. 8, 1782, *Works of JA*, 7:572–73, 634, 646–48.

35. British informant, The Hague, Sept. 27, 1782, PRO, FO 37/4.

36. *Works of JA*, 7:48 n.

37. Adams to Livingston, ibid., 7:525; for the May 1, 1781, letter to Vauguyon, see ibid., p. 409.

38. Vergennes to Luzerne, CP-EU, vol. 15.

39. *Journals of the Continental Congress*, 20:769, 779–80.

40. Luzerne to Vergennes, Aug. 24, 1781; Vergennes to Luzerne, Dec. 24, 1781, CP-EU, vols. 18, 19; Vergennes to Vauguyon, Aug. 29, 1782; Vauguyon to Vergennes, Aug. 20, 1782, CP-H, vol. 550.

41. *Boston Patriot*, April 20, 24, 1811; Vauguyon to Vergennes, May 7, 1782, CP-H, vol. 549; British informant, The Hague, May 3, 1782, PRO, FO 37/4.

42. Vauguyon to Vergennes, June 17, 1782; Vergennes to Vauguyon, June 23, 1782, CP-H, vol. 549.

43. Vauguyon to Vergennes, July 16, 1782; Vergennes to Vauguyon, July 21, 1782; Vauguyon to Vergennes, Aug. 20, 1782, ibid., vol. 550.

44. Morris, *The Peacemakers*, p. 304.

45. To the President of Congress, Aug. 18, 1782, Adams Papers, microfilm ed., reel 106.

46. *Boston Patriot*, May 25, 1811.

47. *Works of JA*, 7:641.

Chapter 6

1. *Works of JA,* 7:492-93, 528; *Adams Family Correspondence,* 4:323; Adams Papers, microfilm ed., reel 107.

2. To Edmund Jenings, July 20, 1782, Adams Papers, microfilm ed., reel 357; Butterfield, *Diary and Autobiography,* 3:40 n; *Works of JA,* 7:627.

3. Adams to Livingston, Adams Papers, microfilm ed., reel 110; Butterfield, *Diary and Autobiography,* 3:48 n, 47.

4. Adams to Ridley, Sept. 29, 1782, Adams Papers, microfilm ed., reel 107; *Boston Patriot,* May 11, 1811; Butterfield, *Diary and Autobiography,* 3:38.

5. Frank Monaghan, ed., *The Diary of John Jay during the Peace Negotiations of 1782* (New Haven, Conn., 1934), p. 14.

6. Morris, *The Peacemakers,* chapt. 14; Bemis, *Diplomacy,* pp. 217–20.

7. Monaghan, *Diary of John Jay,* p. 13.

8. Butterfield, *Diary and Autobiography,* 3:47.

9. *Works of JA,* 8:5.

10. Butterfield, *Diary and Autobiography,* 3:64–65, 83.

11. Gordon O. Rothney, "British Policy in the North American Cod-Fisheries, 1775–1819" (Ph.D. diss., University of London, 1950), pp. 55–60; Fitzherbert to Grantham, Aug. 21, 1782; Grantham to Fitzherbert, Sept. 3, 1782, PRO, FO 27/3.

12. Butterfield, *Diary and Autobiography,* 3:83–84.

13. To Livingston, Nov. 11, 1782, *Works of JA,* 8:7.

14. To Edmund Jenings, April 18, 1783, Adams Papers, microfilm ed., reel 108; see also Butterfield, *Diary and Autobiography,* 3:116; to Livingston, July 10, 14, 1783, *Works of JA,* 8:90, 98–99.

15. On France's desire that Canada remain in British hands to promote American dependence, see Corwin, *French Policy,* p. 233; Stinchcombe, *The American Revolution,* p. 27; Morris, *The Peacemakers,* p. 326. On Adams's ignorance of French intentions vis-à-vis Canada, see, for example, his letters to A. M. Cerisier, Oct. 23, 1780; to William Lee, Dec. 6, 1780, Adams Papers, microfilm ed., reel 102.

16. Butterfield, *Diary and Autobiography,* 3: 39 n.

17. Ibid., p. 82. Some historians have found Franklin's statement

"inexplicable." Shaw, *The Character of John Adams*, pp. 169-70. I find it puzzling because of its superfluity. The Doctor, by declining to communicate to Vergennes his peace proposals to Richard Oswald of July 10, 1782, and by joining Jay in withholding from the count the terms negotiated with Oswald on Oct. 5, 1782, had long since violated the instruction of June 15, 1781. Why did he create the impression on October 30 that he was preparing to embark on a course that he had pursued for months? He may have been trying to advertise to the British a "split" between France and America to encourage their generosity. Bemis, *Diplomacy*, pp. 208-9; Morris, *The Peacemakers*, p. 346.

18. *Boston Patriot*, July 27, 1811.
19. Wharton, *Diplomatic Correspondence*. 5:807.
20. Oswald to Thomas Townsend, Oct. 7, 1782, PRO, FO 27/2; Cabinet minute, Oct. 17, 1782, *The Correspondence of King George the Third*, ed. John Fortescue, 6 vols. (London, 1927–1928), 6:143–44. Strachey's Instructions, Oct. 20, 1782, are in *Appendix to the Sixth Report of the Royal Commission on Historical Manuscripts*, p. 403; *Boston Patriot*, July 31, 1811.
21. Bemis, *Diplomacy*, pp. 207-9.
22. Oswald, minute, Oct. 11, 1782; Oswald to Townsend, Oct. 7, 1782, PRO, FO 27/2.
23. See Vincent T. Harlow, *The Founding of the Second British Empire*, 2 vols. (London, 1951), 1:326-27, 334, 340, 393–400, for the Franco-British negotiations on the Newfoundland fishing problem during 1782–1783. See also pp. 327 n, 397.
24. Bemis, *Diplomacy*, p. 231. For a contrary view, see Harlow, *Founding of the Second British Empire*, 1:289.
25. Butterfield, *Diary and Autobiography*, 3:38, 82.
26. Ibid., pp. 43–44; Oswald to Townsend, Nov. 6, 1782, PRO, FO 27/2; Butterfield, *Diary and Autobiography*, 3:46.
27. Butterfield, *Diary and Autobiography*, 3:40 n, 50 n; *Boston Patriot*, Nov. 13, 1811.
28. Oswald, Observations concerning the Fishery, Nov. 8, 1782, PRO, FO 27/2.
29. Morris, *The Peacemakers*, pp. 350–51.
30. Wharton, *Diplomatic Correspondence*, 5:852.
31. See Morris, *The Peacemakers*, pp. 367–81.

32. Strachey to Townsend, Nov. 8, 1782, PRO, FO 27/2; Cabinet minute, Nov. 11, 1782, in *Correspondence of George the Third*, 6:155; the Americans were to be kept at fifteen leagues' distance from Cape Breton. Oswald to Townsend, Nov. 30, 1782, PRO, FO 27/2; Morris, *The Peacemakers*, p. 378.

33. To Livingston, Dec. 4, 1782, *Works of JA*, 8:16; to Abigail Adams, July 1, 1782, *Adams Family Correspondence*, 4:338; to Abigail Adams, Dec. 28, 1782, Feb. 18, 1783; to Thomas McKean, Feb. 6, 1783, Adams Papers, microfilm ed., reel 108.

34. Adams to Dumas, Adams Papers, microfilm ed., reel 108; *Warren-Adams Letters*, 2:206-7; to Abigail Adams, Feb. 26, 1783, Adams Papers, microfilm ed., reel 108.

35. *Warren-Adams Letters*, 2:205; to Abigail Adams, Feb. 26, 27, 1783, Adams Papers, microfilm ed., reel 108.

36. To James Warren, March 20, April 9, 12, 1783; to William Gordon, April 15, 1783; to Abigail Adams, Feb. 18, 1783, Adams Papers, microfilm ed., reel 108.

37. To Abigail Adams, April 16, 1783, ibid., reel 360; Butterfield, *Diary and Autobiography*, 3:103; to Abigail Adams, Feb. 27, 1783; to Thomas McKean, Feb. 6, 1783, Adams Papers, microfilm ed., reel 108.

38. To Livingston, Nov. 6, 1782, *Works of JA*, 7:659-60; Butterfield, *Diary and Autobiography*, 3:50, 53; to William Lee, April 6, 1783, Adams Papers, microfilm ed., reel 108; Butterfield, *Diary and Autobiography*, 3:89; Adams to Livingston, May 25, 1783, Adams Papers, microfilm ed., reel 108; see also Adams to James Warren, April 13, 1783, ibid.

39. To Livingston, Feb. 5, 1783, *Works of JA*, 8:34; Butterfield, *Diary and Autobiography*, 3:64-65, 105, 116; to Abigail Adams, Feb. 26, 27, 1783, Adams Papers, microfilm ed., reel 108.

40. Irving Brant, *James Madison*, 5 vols. (Indianapolis, Ind., 1948), 2:141-45. Stinchcombe, *The American Revolution*, p. 174, cites a self-serving letter by Barbé-Marbois to establish a claim for French influence on Madison's activities.

41. To James Warren, March 21, 1783, *Warren-Adams Letters*, 2:197.

42. Butterfield, *Diary and Autobiography*, 3:38, 100; to Livingston, Nov. 8, 1782, *Works of JA*, 8:4; to James Warren, March 21, 1783, *Warren-Adams Letters*, 2:197; *Works of JA*, 7:628; to Wil-

liam Gordon, April 15, 1783, Adams Papers, microfilm ed., reel 108; Butterfield, *Diary and Autobiography*, 3:64, 81; Wharton, *Diplomatic Correspondence*, 6:692–93; *Warren-Adams Letters*, 2:198.

43. To William Lee, Adams Papers, microfilm ed., reel 108; to James Warren, April 13, 1783, *Warren-Adams Letters*, 2:211, 210.

44. To Livingston, Nov. 8, 1782, *Works of JA*, 8:5; Butterfield, *Diary and Autobiography*, 3:118.

45. Gilbert Chinard, *Honest John Adams* (Boston, 1933), pp. 178–79; Shaw, *The Character of John Adams*, p. 183.

46. To Samuel Osgood, April 12, 1783, Adams Papers, microfilm ed., reel 108.

47. To James Warren, April 13, 1783, *Warren-Adams Letters*, 2:209–10; to Livingston, May 25, 1783, Adams Papers, microfilm ed., reel 108; to Warren, April 13, 1783, *Warren-Adams Letters*, 2:211; to Edmund Jenings, April 18, 1783, Adams Papers, microfilm ed., reel 108.

48. Franklin to Laurens, Princeton University Library, Princeton, N.J.

49. *Writings of Franklin*, 9:62.

50. Butterfield, *The Book of Abigail and John*, pp. 370–73.

51. *Boston Patriot*, Feb. 1, 1812.

52. Shaw, *The Character of John Adams*, pp. 186–91.

53. To Livingston, June 16, 1783, Adams Papers, microfilm ed., reel 108. Adams, to be precise, received a copy of a congressional resolution; the commission, authorizing the appointment, arrived some months later. To Warren, Sept. 10, 1783, ibid.; see also letters to Elias Boudinot, Sept. 8, 1783; to Abigail Adams, Sept. 7, 1783; to Livingston, July 9, 1783; to Henry Laurens, July 12, 1783, ibid., reels 107, 108; Butterfield, *Diary and Autobiography*, 3:144; Morris, *The Peacemakers*, p. 520 n. 25.

54. *Warren-Adams Letters*, 2:222; Adams to Osgood, June 30, 1784; to Gerry, Sept. 10, 1783; to Arthur Lee, Jan. 31, 1785, Adams Papers, microfilm ed., reel 107; *Boston Patriot*, March 7, 1812; Butterfield, *Diary and Autobiography*, 3:103; Adams to Warren, April 13, 1783, *Warren-Adams Letters*, 2:211; to Gerry, June 27, 1784, Adams Papers, microfilm ed., reel 107; to Warren, Sept. 10, 1783, *Warren-Adams Letters*, 2:222.

55. To Osgood, June 30, 1784; to William Carmichael, April 22,

1784; to Gerry, May 2, 1785, Adams Papers, microfilm ed., reels 107, 364.

56. To Osgood, June 30, 1784; to Ridley, Jan. 25, 1784; to Arthur Lee, April 6, 1784, ibid., reel 107.

57. To Livingston, July 14, 1783, *Works of JA*, 8:97; to Gerry, Sept. 10, 1783, Adams Papers, microfilm ed., reel 107.

58. Butterfield, *Diary and Autobiography*, 3:103; see also Adams to Gerry, June 27, 1784; to Osgood, June 30, 1784; to Thomas McKean, Feb. 6, 1783, Adams Papers, microfilm ed., reels 107, 108.

59. To Thomas Barclay, May 12, 1784, Adams Papers, microfilm ed., reel 107.

60. To Jackson, June 16, 1784, ibid.

61. To Lee, Jan. 31, 1785, ibid.

62. Reply to Hamilton, 1800, ibid., reel 399; to Rush, April 12, 1809, *Old Family Letters*, p. 232; *Boston Patriot*, May 18, 1811; to Rush, June 23, 1807, *Old Family Letters*, p. 148; to Abigail Adams, Jan. 9, 1797, Adams Papers, microfilm ed., reel 383.

63. *Correspondence of the Late President Adams*, pp. 82–83; to Rush, Dec. 4, 1805, *Old Family Letters*, p. 88; Elbridge Gerry, President's Conference, March 26, 1799, Gerry Papers, Library of Congress; Reply to Hamilton, 1800, Adams Papers, microfilm ed., reel 399.

64. See Hutson, "Origins of 'The Paranoid Style.' "

65. Kentucky Resolutions, 1798, Thomas Jefferson, *The Works of Thomas Jefferson*, ed. Paul L. Ford, 12 vols. (New York, 1904–1905), 8:474; Andrew Jackson, Second Inaugural Address, March 4, 1833, James D. Richardson, ed., *A Compilation of the Messages and Papers of the Presidents*, 20 vols. (New York, 1897–1917), 3:1223; "Farewell Address," March 4, 1837, Harold C. Syrett, *Andrew Jackson: His Contribution to the American Tradition* (Indianapolis, Ind., 1953), pp. 261–62.

66. Hutson, "Origins of 'The Paranoid Style' "; Marshall Smelser, "The Jacobin Phrenzy: The Menace of Monarchy, Plutocracy, and Anglophilia, 1789–1798," *Review of Politics* 21 (January 1959): 241; "The Jacobin Phrenzy: Federalism and the Menace of Liberty, Equality, and Fraternity," ibid., 13 (October 1951): 457–58. See also Banning, "Republican Ideology," pp. 183–84.

Chapter 7

1. Bailyn, *Ideological Origins*, pp. 56 ff.
2. Bernard Bailyn, "The Central Themes of the American Revolution," in *Essays on the American Revolution*, ed. Stephen G. Kurtz and James H. Hutson (Chapel Hill, N.C., 1973), p. 9; Isaac Kramnick, *Bolingbroke and His Circle: The Politics of Nostalgia in the Age of Walpole* (Cambridge, Mass., 1968), pp. 123–25, 148 ff.
3. Bailyn, *Ideological Origins*, pp. 70–79; Corwin, "The Progress of Constitutional Theory between the Declaration of Independence and the Meeting of the Philadelphia Convention," *American Historical Review* 30 (April 1925): 535.
4. Gilbert, *To the Farewell Address*, pp. 54, 56, 66, 87, 89, 85–89; Wharton, *Diplomatic Correspondence*, 1:253, 263, 289, 513.
5. Gilbert, *To the Farewell Address*, pp. 56-69.
6. Montesquieu might be considered a philosophe, but of this there is considerable doubt. Stourzh claims that Montesquieu influenced early American foreign policy in an idealistic direction, but his description of Montesquieu's foreign-policy ideas makes it appear that the Frenchman considered trade as a source of power, as did the mercantilists and other power politicians, at least as often as he did as an instrument of international comity. Gerald Stourzh, *Alexander Hamilton and the Idea of Republican Government* (Stanford, Calif., 1970), pp. 140–48.
7. *Notes on Virginia*, in *The Life and Selected Writings of Thomas Jefferson*, ed. Adrienne Koch and William Peden (New York, 1944), p. 215.
8. *Old Family Letters*, p. 120; see also Adams to John Jay, Feb. 26, 1786; to John Thaxter, April 8, 1777, Adams Papers, microfilm ed., reels 112, 91.
9. Hutson, *A Decent Respect to the Opinions of Mankind*, pp. 54, 105. In January 1776 members of Congress, formulating proposals for reconciliation with Great Britain, pledged, on one occasion, that "the Navigation Act will remain inviolate" and, on another, that Americans would "confirm, if it be required, by perpetual Acts of their Legislatures the Acts commonly called the Acts of Navigation." Lord Drummond's Minutes, Jan. 10–11, 1776; John

Dickinson, "Proposed Instructions for Commissioners to Negotiate Peace with Great Britain," Jan. 9–24, 1776. Smith, *Letters of Delegates to Congress*, 3:64–71, 74–76.

10. Smith, *Letters of Delegates to Congress*, 4:166.

11. For the text of the Model Treaty, see *Journals of the Continental Congress*, 5:768–78.

12. Wood, *Creation of the American Republic*.

13. For a lucid exposition of the antithesis Americans and English Opposition writers perceived between commerce and virtue, see J. G. A. Pocock, "Virtue and Commerce in the Eighteenth Century," *Journal of Interdisciplinary History* 1 (1972): 119–34; Adams to Benjamin Rush, Dec. 28, 1807, *Old Family Letters*, p. 176; Wood, *Creation of the American Republic*, p. 94; *Warren-Adams Letters*, 1:222–23, 2:187; to Gerry, Adams Papers, microfilm ed., reel 111.

14. Dalton to John Adams, July 21, 1785, Adams Papers, microfilm ed., reel 365; Silas to Simeon Deane, May 16, 1781, Deane Papers, New-York Historical Society, *Collections* (1889), pp. 336, 341.

15. Gilbert, *To the Farewell Address*, pp. 60–66; Gabriel Bonnot, Abbe de Mably, *Remarks Concerning the Government and the Laws of the United States of America* (Dublin, 1785), pp. 173–85; Gabriel Riquetti, Comte de Mirabeau, *Considerations on the Order of Cincinnatus* (London, 1785), pp. 214 ff.; Raynal, "An Address to the Independent Citizens of America," *Lloyd's Evening Post*, Dec. 22–28, 1785. My attention was drawn to the views of these writers on the relationship of commerce and republicanism by an excellent manuscript by Gerald J. Ghelfi, "European Opinions of American Republicanism during the 'Critical Period,' 1781–1789"; Mably, *Remarks*, pp. 184–85.

16. *Notes on Virginia*; Jefferson to Gerry, May 13, 1797, Koch and Peden, *Life and Writings of Thomas Jefferson*, pp. 285, 543; Adams to John Jay, Dec. 6, 1785, Adams Papers, microfilm ed., reel 111.

17. Jefferson to Charles Van Hogendorp, Oct. 13, 1785, Koch and Peden, *Life and Writings of Thomas Jefferson*, p. 384; Adams to Jay, Dec. 6, 1785, Adams Papers, microfilm ed., reel 111.

18. To Robert Livingston, Feb. 21, 1782, Wharton, *Diplomatic Corre-*

spondence, 5:196; for the term militia diplomacy, see Bemis, *Diplomacy*, p. 114 n; Stourzh, *Benjamin Franklin*, pp. 126, 159–61; *Adams Family Correspondence*, 3:395 n; Mary B. Foley, "The Triumph of Militia Diplomacy: John Adams in the Netherlands, 1780–1782" (Ph.D. diss., Loyola Univerity of Chicago, 1968); Alonzo Dill, "William Lee: Militia Diplomat," Virginia Independence Bicentennial Commission publication, forthcoming.

19. Wharton, *Diplomatic Correspondence*, 1:512.
20. Ibid., 2:156–57, 226, 119.
21. Butterfield, *Diary and Autobiography*, 4:71.
22. Memorial to the States General, April 19, 1781, Wharton, *Diplomatic Correspondence*, 4:372.
23. Butterfield, *Diary and Autobiography*, 4:44–45; Wilson to Morris, Jan. 14, 1777, New Jersey Historical Society.
24. Wharton, *Diplomatic Correspondence*, 1:511; Butterfield, *Diary and Autobiography*, 4:146; Adams to Treasury Board, Sept. 19, 1779, Adams Papers, microfilm ed., reel 93; Butterfield, *Diary and Autobiography*, 4:109; Adams to Abigail Adams, Nov. 27, 1778, Adams Papers, microfilm ed., reel 93.
25. Butterfield, *Diary and Autobiography*, 4:231.
26. Adams to John Jay, May 16, 1786, Adams Papers, microfilm ed., reels 112, 111.
27. Wharton, *Diplomatic Correspondence*, 1:513–14.

A NOTE ON SOURCES

The basic source for a study of John Adams is, of course, his own papers, which are available in a microfilm edition, prepared under the auspices of the Massachusetts Historical Society, in many major research libraries. Charles Francis Adams's edition of his grandfather's papers, *The Works of John Adams*, 10 vols. (Boston, 1850–1856), has been superseded in the past twenty years by the distinguished editions prepared by Lyman Butterfield and his colleagues and by Butterfield's successor, Robert Taylor: *Diary and Autobiography of John Adams*, 4 vols. (Cambridge, Mass., 1961); *Adams Family Correspondence*, 4 vols. (Cambridge, Mass., 1963–1973); *The Adams Papers: The Papers of John Adams*, 2 vols. to date (Cambridge, Mass., 1977–).

The papers of many of Adams's colleagues are available in modern editions: *The Papers of Thomas Jefferson*, ed. Julian P. Boyd et al., 19 vols. to date (Princeton, 1950–); *The Papers of Benjamin Franklin*, ed. Leonard W. Labaree et al., 21 vols. to date (New Haven, Conn., 1959–); *The Papers of Alexander Hamilton*, ed. Harold Syrett, 26 vols. (New York, 1961–1979). Since the Labaree-Willcox edition of Franklin's papers has not reached the years of Adams's diplomatic career, two additional multivolume editions should be consulted: *The Complete Works of Benjamin Franklin*, ed. John Bigelow, 10 vols. (New York, 1887–1888), and *The Writings of Benjamin Franklin*, ed. Albert H. Smyth, 10 vols. (New York, 1905–1907). An indispensable, but occasionally unreliable, source is *The Revolutionary Diplomatic Correspondence of the United States*, ed. Francis Wharton, 6 vols. (Washington, D.C., 1889). Wharton should be supplemented by *Letters of Delegates to Congress 1774–1789*, ed. Paul H. Smith et al., 3 vols. to date (Washington, D.C., 1976–), and by *Letters of Members of the Continental Congress*, ed. Edmund C. Burnett, 8 vols. (Washington, D.C., 1921–1936).

Note on Sources

The records of French diplomacy are housed in the Ministère des Affaires Etrangères, Paris. Correspondance politique, Etats-Unis and Hollande, should be consulted for the appropriate years. Transcripts of much of the relevant French Etats-Unis documentation are held by the Library of Congress. Selected French sources are published in Henri Doniol, *Histoire de la participation de la France a l'etablissement des Etats-Unis d'Amerique*, 5 vols. (Paris, 1884–1892). Some records also appear in *Facsimiles of Manuscripts in European Archives Relating to America 1773-1783*, ed. B. F. Stevens, 25 vols. (London, 1889).

Of the recent Adams biographies the most detailed is Page Smith, *John Adams*, 2 vols. (Garden City, N.Y., 1962). A superb interpretive study, of which all students of Adams must take account, is Peter Shaw, *The Character of John Adams* (Chapel Hill, N.C., 1976).

The monographic literature on the diplomacy of the Revolution is vast. Samuel F. Bemis's *The Diplomacy of the American Revolution* (New York, 1935) has retained its authority. It must be supplemented, however, by Richard B. Morris's magisterial *The Peacemakers* (New York, 1965). Although I disagree with the author's thesis, Felix Gilbert's *To the Farewell Address: Ideas of Early American Foreign Policy* (Princeton, N.J., 1961) cannot be ignored by students of the period. The following three recent monographs are exceptionally informative and well executed: William Stinchcombe, *The American Revolution and the French Alliance* (Syracuse, N.Y., 1969); Jonathan Dull, *The French Navy and American Independence* (Princeton, N.J., 1975); and Lawrence S. Kaplan, *Colonies into Nations: American Diplomacy, 1763-1801* (New York, 1972). An article that should not be neglected (because it is the best treatment in English of Vergennes) is Orville T. Murphy, "Charles Gravier de Vergennes: Profile of an Old Regime Diplomat," *Political Science Quarterly* 83 (Sept. 1968): 400–18.

INDEX

Index

Index

Index